River Cafe London

Thirty Years of Recipes and the
Story of a Much-Loved Restaurant

Ruth Rogers
Rose Gray
Sian Wyn Owen
Joseph Trivelli

Matthew Donaldson
Jean Pigozzi
Stephanie Nash
Anthony Michael

With a Foreword by
April Bloomfield

Alfred A. Knopf
New York
2018

Foreword

My years at The River Cafe were incredibly special to me. Rose Gray and Ruthie Rogers not only taught me how to cook, but how to be the kind of chef I wanted to be. I learned to do things differently, to be flexible and to adapt, and, most important, to enjoy what I was doing. They taught me to appreciate the simplicity of a dish, even when an immense amount of planning and work went into it.

They set me on the path to become the chef I am today.

I am excited to have this beautiful, inspiring book from Ruthie Rogers, Sian Wyn Owen and Joseph Trivelli. I love how it draws you into their family with photographs that show the space and stories that tell the history of the restaurant. It is a joy to see their classic recipes updated, and to discover some new ones along the way. The great thing about The River Cafe is that it is always growing, refreshing and fun, with a buzzy atmosphere and the feeling that you are a part of something truly special.

This book, with its bold graphics and bright colors, is like an invitation to eat at one of the best restaurants in the world.

I hope *River Cafe London* will change your life the way working at The River Cafe changed mine.

April Bloomfield

Introduction

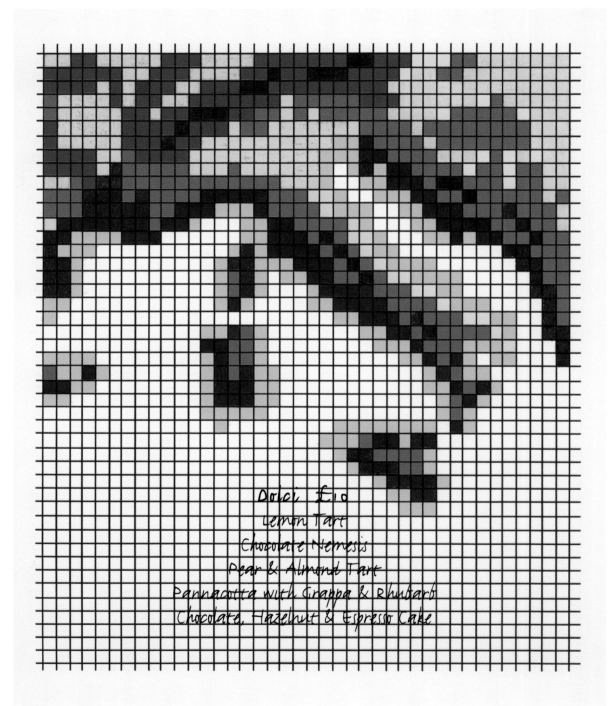

Dolci £10
Lemon Tart
Chocolate Nemesis
Pear & Almond Tart
Pannacotta with Grappa & Rhubarb
Chocolate, Hazelnut & Espresso Cake

Reinhard Voigt

The Book

Change is timeless. A good restaurant is alive. It lives, it grows and so do its recipes.

In the twenty-two years since we wrote our first cookbook or "the blue book," as it has become known, much has changed—the way we eat, the way we shop and the way we cook. There has been an explosion in the availability of ingredients. Vegetables arrive daily from the Milan market, mozzarella is flown in from Naples, people grow herbs in their window boxes and salad leaves in their gardens.

Everyone is a chef.

Our first book, *The River Cafe Cookbook*, was written originally to be a manual for our own chefs to follow. But, as chefs, we have grown as well. We have traveled all over Italy, from Piemonte to Sicily, discovering new ingredients, new methods and, most of all, new people to expand our knowledge of the food we love. So, in thirty years, our book has changed.

To celebrate our thirtieth birthday, we returned to our first recipes in the blue book. Here we share our knowledge and experience of how we have refined those classic dishes.

Mixed in with the revisited classics are more than thirty new recipes created through our work and travels together: Mezze Paccheri, Black Pepper and Langoustine, an eccentric combination of langoustines with Pecorino; White Asparagus with Bottarga Butter, a variation on the classic anchovy sauce; and Crab and Raw Artichoke Salad.

The design of *River Cafe London*, by Anthony Michael and Stephanie Nash, is inspired by the bold art, architecture and bright colors of the restaurant—the pink wood oven, the yellow pass, the blue carpet. The Joseph Albers font, throughout the book, reflects these qualities.

Matthew Donaldson photographed the food on sunny days in our garden. Jean Pigozzi, who took the dynamic black-and-white photographs of the restaurant in action for our first book, returned to capture the customers, chefs and waiters who are the River Cafe family.

River Cafe London is the story of a restaurant that began with two unknown chefs and a space large enough for nine tables.

We have grown. We have a new vision, but the same conclusion: with good ingredients and a strong tradition, change and recipes can be timeless.

The Artists

In 1991, Ellsworth Kelly drew a still life on the
back of a River Cafe menu and, on another,
a self-portrait, looking in the mirror of the
men's bathroom.

Cy Twombly, in his distinctive hand, wrote
"I love lunch with Ruthie" on a menu, after a
long Sunday lunch celebrating his exhibition
at the Serpentine Gallery in 2004.

For this book, we asked the artists in the
River Cafe's extended family to draw or
paint on a menu.

There is a connection between art and
food, and these works are unmistakably an
expression of each artist.

We love cooking for them:

Peter Doig, Susan Elias, Damien Hirst,
Brice Marden, Michael Craig Martin,
Ed Ruscha, Reinhard Voigt, Jonas Wood.

We thank them for making *River Cafe London*
a more beautiful book.

Richard Bryant

The River Cafe

So, how did it all begin thirty years ago?

In March of 1987, Rose Gray and I met for a coffee. I wanted to tell her about a space that had come up in Thames Wharf where Richard Rogers and Partners had just bought a group of warehouses to convert into offices for their architectural practice.

We met on the Kings Road at Drummonds, which today is McDonald's—so you could say that The River Cafe was actually conceived in a McDonald's. After the coffee, we went to look at the space available. There were three floor-to-ceiling windows facing south over the Thames and room enough for nine tables. There was a communal green space in the middle. We imagined a vegetable and herb garden. We fell in love with the place, in love with the idea.

And so it began.

Rose, Richard and I became partners. Richard did the drawings, the lights came from The Reject Shop, chairs from Habitat and secondhand ovens from a yard in Coventry. Rose's husband, the sculptor David MacIlwaine, who worked with wire, designed our logo. My brother Michael had our menus printed onto baseball caps, which he sent us from L.A. My sister Susan's paintings were on the walls.

We called it The River Cafe. The imaginary garden became real and we planted wild arugula, the seeds brought home from a holiday in Tuscany. Our children worked with us—Rose's and mine.

Bo was three at the time.

It was a family affair.

If restrictions can drive creativity, then we definitely had ours. The Hammersmith planners allowed us to be open only at lunchtime and available only to the architects, designers, model makers and framers who worked in the warehouses—people who usually had nothing but a sandwich for their lunch.

This is how we began—on a site that was previously an oil depository.

We made hamburgers, but with mayonnaise using extra virgin olive oil, and sandwiches with taleggio. We also made Pappa Pomodoro, which no one ate. As one customer said, "I'm not paying £3.50 for some stale bread and tomatoes." We grilled squid and put it with arugula and fresh red chile. It has been on the menu ever since. We found a recipe for a cake and called it Chocolate Nemesis.

The only thing we didn't make was money. With every sandwich and leftover soup our overdraft increased. How long could we survive? The worst day was when a young woman came on her bicycle selling sandwiches to all the offices for 25 pence cheaper than ours. We told her she was trespassing and asked her to leave.

Actually, we were treated as trespassers. A petition was sent to the council, signed by 100 people, complaining, "The River Cafe and its clientele are seriously diminishing the tone of the area." Fortunately, we also had our fans. Fay Maschler, the food critic for the *Evening Standard*, wrote a review saying, "I am going to tell you about a restaurant run by two women with no professional experience, miles from anywhere, that you are not allowed to go to."

Word spread. We stopped making sandwiches. We were allowed to open to the public; a year later, to open at night until eleven; a year after that, on the weekends. We became a restaurant.

But The River Cafe is not just about the food and the wine; it is also about the people who come to eat here and the people who work here—the true vital ingredients. I often wonder what happened to the man who asked us to make a cake with the words "will you marry me" and then canceled the cake halfway through the meal; the woman who used her mobile phone on a busy Sunday to call reception to summon a waiter to her table; the television journalist who took her shirt off in the middle of the restaurant because she lost a bet; and the American who wanted a taxi and when I asked where she was going said, "London."

The River Cafe began with family, and it is still a family. The space has grown and the family has grown. Now, Sian Wyn Owen, Joseph Trivelli, Charles Pullan, Vashti Armit and I head a team of 100 brilliant people.

Thirty years later, we are still here in our beautiful garden with our view over the River Thames.

1987

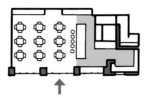

1994

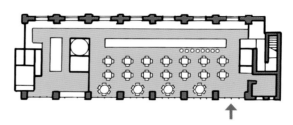

1999

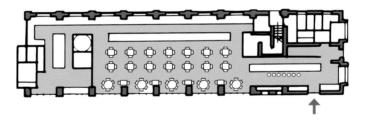

2008

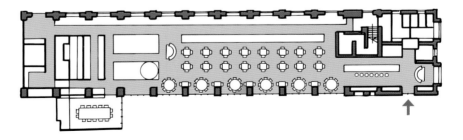

The growth of a restaurant.
Drawings by Stephen Spence

James Bedford

The River Café

Thursday, 15th September

"Papa Pomodoro" - Soup of Tuscan bread, plum tomatoes and fresh basil — £3.00.

Coppa di Parma with a salad of Rocket e Trevisse £3.75.

Artichoke Hearts with French Beans e Tapinade £3.75.

Chargrilled red & yellow Peppers, capers, anchovies, basil and bruschetta. — £3.50

Girolles and Ceps with grilled Polenta e Parmesan £6.50.

Hot Mozzarella, green chilles on Frisée — £3.50.

Penne al Arabiata.   starter £3.00 ; Main £5.00.

Wild Scottish Partridge with pancetta, braised cabbage and bruschetta £14.50.

Pan-fried Calves Liver with Sage and braised endives £8.00.

Grilled Squid with rocket and French Fries £8.50.

Insalata di Manzo with trevisse, rocket e horseradish £8.00

Char-grilled Corn-fed Chicken 'Spago' stuffed with Italian parsley, garlic and french fries £7.75.

    River   Café   Hamburger — £3.75.

Blackberry Tart £3.75   Chevere £2.50.

Pear Tart £3.75   Torta di Gorgonzola.

Strawberry Sorbet £2.50   £3.75.

THAMES WHARF RAINVILLE ROAD
LONDON W6 9HA 01-385 3344

One of our first menus

ent it requires a little time to digest."

"Brain Opera" is an homage of sorts to the work of Machover's mentor, Marvin Minsky, the Yoda-like mega-intellectual who has spent the past forty-odd years examining the relationship between music, our brains, and society. Minsky often asks questions like, Why do we spend so much time on music when it has little or no practical value?

"I think one of the big taboos is this kind of 'right-brain, left-brain' thing," Machover explains. "One of the things that 'Brain Opera' puts on the table is that thinking and feeling are a lot closer than we ever thought—that logic ain't so logical. I find it all very exciting."

• •

RIVER RENAISSANCE

WHAT many people believe is the best Italian restaurant in Europe sits on the Thames in London, in a neighborhood that until recently was a dark province in the empire of fried fish and wilted sandwiches. The restaurant is Ruth Rogers and Rose Gray's River Café; it is in a reclaimed-warehouse space designed by Rogers' husband, the architect Richard Rogers; and not long ago its cooking became the subject of a book, written by Rogers and Gray and entitled "The River Café Cook Book," which, when it appeared in England, last year, was called by one reviewer, flatly, "the best cookery book ever published." Even our own Wolfgang Puck has praised it as "the most delicious Italian cookbook I have ever put my hands on," and anyone who has cooked up Rogers and Gray's *penne alla carbonara* or their *spaghetti al limone* would probably agree, or, anyway, be too busy eating to argue. This month, the book was published in the United States, under the title "Rogers Gray Italian Country Cook Book." (There is a perfectly nice River Café on a barge in the East River, and nobody wants to confuse readers or antagonize its owner.) Both the restaurant and the book are an expression of a renaissance of the London Modern sensibility—the century-old William Morris-to-Rayner Banham sensibility, which insists that a faith in common sense, clean lines, English river air, and imported Mediterranean folk culture will make England young again.

The other evening at the River Café, Ruth Rogers talked a little about the origins of the restaurant and the book as she stood

not far from the pure interior's only decoration, a giant projected-shadow clock. On this night, there was a nice mix of improbable types—movie people (Steve Martin is a regular); art people (Lucian Freud is, too); and a sprinkling of Saatchis—but mostly it was filled with ordinary people out for a good dinner. It is a casually democratic restaurant, and Rogers sometimes has to spend a lot of energy trying to dissuade visiting Americans (she is American herself) from their conviction that there is a best table in the house, and that they are not at it. "Americans are strange about tables," she said. "The other night I had to say, 'But this is where Richard sits.' " As she spoke, she noticed, with pleasure, that an intense two-year-old had escaped from his parents' table on the restaurant's terrace and had been picked up by a waiter, who was holding him on his hip as the parents watched.

"You see," Rogers went on, "in 1987 Richard and his partners had found these warehouses on the Thames and had the hope that they could become a sort of community. We had a record company, a small architect and designer, even someone making stained glass. Richard tore down one of the warehouses and made a green space, with the vision of having a place to eat for that community. Rose is an old friend, and from the very first discussion we realized that we had the same conception. She had lived for four years with her family near Lucca; I went to Italy every summer, since Richard's family is Italian; and we both wondered why we couldn't have the kind of food here that you eat in Italian homes. Neither of us is a trained cook. We had learned to cook by cooking for our kids,

and we decided to run the whole restaurant on domestic terms, the way we run our lives. We change the menu twice a day by looking in the fridge and seeing what's there. Our zabaglione ice cream is Richard's mother's recipe, from when they were here during the war. When she couldn't get Marsala, she substituted Bristol Cream sherry and rum, and we still do. A lot of people say that our recipes are easy, because we use so few ingredients and most of them come from home."

There are people in London who believe that the renovated warehouse area, with the Café as its heart, is a kind of purposeful demonstration piece on the part of Richard Rogers (Labour's cultural éminence rose)—a vision of what he would like London to be in the next century. People think that he wants to show how wonderful the city would be if it were opened to the river, as it hasn't been since Shakespeare's time. A new balance would be struck between the north and south banks, and there would, of course, be a powerful Italian influence everywhere—the full Elizabethan recipe, in fact, which someone mislaid in the seventeenth century. Ruth Rogers deflects the suggestion, though she says she is glad that London is beginning to reclaim its river. "Well, it would be nice if this place could be a model for something, though I would love it if more places like this opened on the river and oh, my God, I think now the baby is serving cappuccino to the customers." Then she laughed, because he was. ♦

"Baby Lamm," John Heilemann; "Damned Glad to Finance You," James Traub; "Mind Games," Andrew Essex; "River Renaissance," Adam Gopnik.

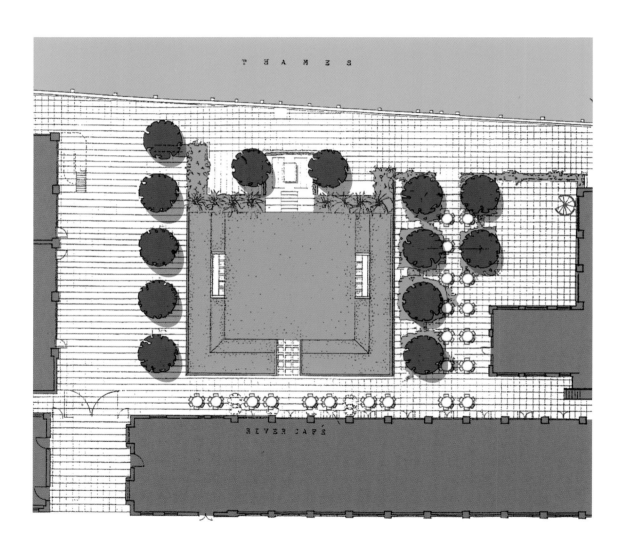

Original plans for the garden
by Georgie Wolton, 1987

Rose Gray

Rose is in The River Cafe, in everything we do.

She is in the way we season the lamb before we put it on the grill. She's there in the way we roll out our pasta dough and slow-cook our vegetables. She's in the yellow color of the kitchen pass and the white tulips at the end of the bar. All this, and more, keeps Rose alive.

The first time I met Rose was in London in 1969. I was tagging along with a friend who had to drop something off at her house. We were shown into a room full of people. And then Rose entered. She had long red hair, a drink in one hand and a baby on her hip. I saw her and the room became different. "Who are you?" she asked me. This was Rose: presence, confidence and unedited directness.

Rose brought excitement, energy, curiosity, glamour and grace to our lives. She had posed for a photograph with a cigarette dangling from her lips and had acted in a movie. She had traveled with her husband, David, to Sri Lanka, Morocco and Mexico.

Rose moved to a farmhouse in the hills above Lucca in 1976 with her family. There, she immersed herself in the food of the region, created an Italian vegetable garden, learned how to make penne arrabbiata from the cook in her village bar and fresh pasta from the woman who came to help in the house. In the pasta chapter, you can see her drawings.

Rose's conviction always convinced me. On one of our first wine trips with David Gleave, she said, "Ruthie, this wine tastes of chocolate and cigarette smoke. What do you think?" I replied, "Rose, this wine tastes of chocolate and cigarette smoke."

Rose didn't like the story about The River Cafe's first days as a staff canteen. In her far-seeing, ambitious mind, we were always going to be the best Italian restaurant of our own, uncompromising, conception. She told a journalist two years after we opened, "Getting Italian Restaurant of the Year isn't good for us. Just today, two people came in who had read about us and because there was only one pasta on the menu left in a fury. Frankly, I was thrilled to see them go."

I miss the judgments passed in Rose's gravelly drawl. She said what she thought, and there was little editing. Too original and, above all, too independent, she seemed to have a phobia of being "impressed" by people.

David Loftus

A grand winemaker once told me it took two olive trees to make a bottle of olive oil. I reported this back to Rose. "He is a liar," she said.

My partner was competitive. I knew I could ruin her day simply by telling her I had had a good meal in another restaurant. At a restaurant considered one of the best in Piemonte, I asked Rose what she thought of the food. She answered in a loud serious voice, "I think the chef really needs to learn how to make polenta."

How many times did I want to say to the recipient of one of Rose's comments, "She didn't really mean it"? But I didn't. Because she did.

Rose was a visionary, a forward-thinker who pushed the boundaries: we should serve mozzarella with nothing else on the plate; we should serve fava beans that you pod yourself; we should have a cheese room; let's grow borlotti beans in Hammersmith; why not create a cocktail and call it the Telefonino?

She broke barriers and had a disregard for the rules. On the way back from one of our many wine trips to Italy, Rose smuggled a fresh cotechino sausage through customs. She was stopped. She claimed it was for her dying mother. Then there was the pumpkin, more than half a meter in diameter, that she saw at Selvapiana Vineyard and had to have. The pumpkin traveled to London in a business-class seat. We sat in economy. People might try to resist but ended up doing what Rose told them to do—either from exhaustion or the realization that she was right.

In an interview Rose once said, "Growing herbs is essential for a civilized life in the city." In those words, Rose is concerned, above all, not with food but with what it means to be civilized. And life, by and large, caught up with Rose's vision for it.

Getting into a black cab in the early days, anywhere in London, Rose would simply say, "Take us to The River Cafe," and I would pray that the driver, for his own sake, would not have to ask where it was. Thirty years later, I think of her every time I say the same words and I don't need to follow with an explanation of where it is.

Our staff got the same tough love, but it was love—uncompromising love. If they did something she didn't approve of, Rose spoke to them as if they were wayward children in an extended family. She was passionate about food and passionate about sharing her knowledge with everyone who wanted to learn. She was an extraordinary teacher.

Although people often tell stories about Rose's, shall we say, "direct approach" and strong opinions, what I remember most about my partner was her gentleness and sweet patience. I can hear her now explaining how to cut a piece of Parmesan, prep a leaf of cicoria (chickory) and describe in minute detail after a wine trip how Vin Santo is made. I can see her demonstrating how to park a car and wear a skirt.

If we at The River Cafe are better chefs, waiters, kitchen porters, sommeliers, managers or, indeed, car parkers and skirt wearers, we can thank Rose Gray.

When, in December 2009, we were awarded an MBE, Rose said, "Ruthie, we are going to wear Chanel suits to the palace." For an ardent anti-establishment rebel, Rose was totally thrilled. David said that she felt proud of the recognition and that she cried.

Seeing how ill Rose was, I suggested that the Palace bring our meeting with the Queen forward from June to February. But when I told Rose she said, "No, no, let's not go then, Ruthie. Let's go in June—I'll be better then . . ."

...

I can still clearly see Rose coming in for her night shift, walking along past the bar, tapping the top of it absent-mindedly as she goes—no hellos, or eye contact, her mind only focused on the menu for that evening.

Rose is still here.
In everything we do.
She always will be.

Ruthie Rogers

Ricotta al Forno
Vignole
Marinated Artichokes
Raw Artichoke Salad
Crab and Raw Artichoke Salad
Bagna Cauda with Prosecco
Bruschetta with Mozzarella and Spinach
White Asparagus with Bottarga Butter
Raw Porcini Salad
Agretti with Tomato and Pangrattato
Zucchini Trifolati
Fig and Cannellini Salad
Chickpea and Fennel Farinata
Panzanella
Red and Yellow Peppers, Anchovies and Capers
Langoustines with Borlotti Beans
Marinated Fresh Anchovies

Antipasti

Ricotta al Forno

Serves 6

unsalted butter and grated Parmesan for the dish

2 handfuls of fresh basil leaves

a handful of fresh mint leaves

a handful of fresh flat-leaf parsley leaves

2¼ cups (500g) bufala ricotta

½ cup (120ml) heavy cream

2 eggs

5 ounces (150g) Parmesan, freshly grated

12 black olives, pitted and chopped

Ricotta al Forno is one of our favorite recipes. A flourless Italian soufflé, when it is ready the top should still wobble.

Preheat the oven to 375°F (190°C).

Using a little butter and some grated Parmesan, coat the bottom and sides of a 12-inch (30cm) round springform pan. Shake out any excess cheese.

Put the herbs into the bowl of a food processor, and put half of the ricotta and cream on the top. Blend until bright green. Add the remainder of the ricotta and cream, and turn on the machine again. While blending, add the eggs, one by one. Season with sea salt and black pepper. Finally, fold in the Parmesan.

Spoon the mixture into the pan and spread the olives over the top. Bake for 20 minutes. The torte should rise and have a brown crust, but still be soft in the center. Serve after 5 minutes.

Vignole

Serves 8

8 small Violetta artichokes with their stalks

juice of 2 lemons

3⅓ pounds (1.5kg) each peas and young fava beans in their pods

4 tablespoons olive oil

2 medium red onions, peeled and finely chopped

2 garlic cloves, peeled and chopped

8 slices prosciutto

2 large handfuls of fresh mint leaves, roughly chopped

½ cup (120ml) extra virgin olive oil, plus extra to serve

8 slices sourdough bread

1 garlic clove, peeled and cut in half

Prepare the artichokes (see Marinated Artichokes, page 35), but leave them whole. Remove the choke with a teaspoon, then cut each artichoke vertically into eight segments. Drop immediately into a bowl of cold water with the lemon juice.

Remove the peas and fava beans from their pods.

In a large pan, heat the olive oil and gently sauté the onions and chopped garlic until starting to soften. Add the artichokes and continue sautéing gently until the onions are translucent. Stirring, add the peas and fava beans. Season and pour in enough water to come about ½ inch (or about 1cm) above the top of the vegetables. Bring to the boil. Lay the slices of prosciutto over the top, cover with a lid and simmer for 20 minutes.

Remove the lid. Lift out the prosciutto and cut into pieces, then return to the pan with the chopped mint and ½ cup (120ml) of extra virgin olive oil. Check for seasoning.

To make the bruschetta, toast the bread on both sides, and gently rub one side only with the garlic halves. Pour on more extra virgin olive oil, then serve the vignole warm or at room temperature with the bruschetta.

Marinated Artichokes

Serves 6

12 small Violetta artichokes with their stalks

juice of 3 lemons

a handful of picked leaves from mixed fresh herbs, to include marjoram, thyme and/or oregano

4 garlic cloves, peeled and thickly sliced

extra virgin olive oil

The Polaroid opposite was taken for one of our earlier books to explain the preparation of an artichoke.

To prepare each artichoke, first cut off some of the stalk, leaving about 2 inches (5cm) attached. Cut or break off the tough outer leaves, starting at the base, until you are left with the pale inner part. Then peel the stalk with a potato peeler, leaving only the pale tender center. Trim the pointed top of the artichoke straight across, which will reveal the choke. Cut the artichoke in half vertically. Remove the choke with a teaspoon. As each artichoke is prepared, drop it into a bowl of cold water with the juice of 2 lemons.

Blanch the artichokes in boiling salted water for about 5 minutes or until the heart is tender. Drain.

Layer the artichoke halves in a large bowl with the herb leaves, garlic and some sea salt and black pepper. Cover completely with extra virgin olive oil and add the remaining lemon juice. Leave to marinate for a minimum of 3 hours.

Raw Artichoke Salad

Serves 6

6 small Violetta artichokes with their stalks

juice of 3 lemons

3 tablespoons extra virgin olive oil, plus extra to drizzle

3½-ounce (100g) piece Parmesan, very thinly shaved

We make this salad only when the artichokes are so fresh you can hear the leaves snap off.

Prepare the artichokes (see Marinated Artichokes, page 35) but leave them whole. Remove the choke with a teaspoon, then finely slice the artichokes vertically and immediately place in a bowl of cold water with the juice of 2 lemons. Set aside.

Make the dressing with the remaining lemon juice and the extra virgin olive oil; season with sea salt and black pepper.

When ready to serve, drain and dry the artichokes and pour the dressing over them. Cover with thin shavings of Parmesan and drizzle over more extra virgin olive oil.

Crab and Raw Artichoke Salad

Serves 2

2 medium Violetta artichokes with their stalks

juice of 1 lemon

7 ounces (200g) white crabmeat

2 teaspoons brown crabmeat

2 tablespoons roughly chopped fresh flat-leaf parsley

2 tablespoons extra virgin olive oil, plus extra to drizzle

We were all together in Venice one summer and had this antipasto at Da Ivo.

Cut the artichokes finely and season them well.

To prepare each artichoke, first cut off some of the stalk, leaving about 2 inches (5cm) attached. Cut or break off the tough outer leaves, starting at the base, until you are left with the pale inner part. Then peel the stalk with a potato peeler, leaving only the pale tender center. Trim the pointed top of the artichoke straight across, which will reveal the choke. Remove the choke with a teaspoon. Slice the artichoke vertically as thinly as possible. As each artichoke is prepared, drop it into a bowl of cold water with half of the lemon juice.

Combine the white and brown crabmeat with the parsley, remaining lemon juice and the extra virgin olive oil. Season with sea salt and black pepper. Drain the artichokes and stir lightly through the crab to combine.

Season again and finish with a drizzle of extra virgin olive oil.

Bagna Cauda with Prosecco

Serves 6

3½ cups (750ml) Prosecco

3 garlic cloves, peeled

10 ounces (300g) Swiss chard

2 fennel bulbs, cut into 6 wedges

6 medium carrots, peeled and cut in half lengthwise

3 celery hearts, quartered

12 salted anchovies

9 ounces (250g) unsalted butter, softened

¼ cup (50ml) olive oil

Put the Prosecco into a saucepan, add the garlic and boil until the Prosecco has reduced to about 7 tablespoons (100ml) and the garlic is soft. Remove from the heat and set aside.

Bring two saucepans of salted water to the boil. In the first pan, blanch the Swiss chard, making sure the stalks are softened before draining. Add the fennel, carrots and celery hearts to the second pan, reduce the heat and simmer for 10 minutes or until tender. Drain.

Rinse the anchovies well under cold running water to remove all the salt, then gently remove the spine bones and heads. Pat dry. Separate the anchovies into fillets.

To finish the sauce, return the saucepan with the reduced Prosecco and softened garlic to the heat, and add the anchovy fillets. Allow them to melt into the mixture. Gently whisk in the softened butter, little by little—remove the pan from the heat after the first addition of butter. When all the butter has been incorporated, add the olive oil and black pepper to taste.

Arrange the warm vegetables on a serving plate. Pour on the sauce and serve immediately.

The River Café

Tuesday 24th May
Antipasti

Prosciutto di Dan Daniele – with new seasons' Charentais Melon
Mozzarella di Bufala – with spring herbs, slow-cooked peas, swiss chard & Selvapiana olive oil
Seppia Nero – Cuttlefish cooked in it's ink with Soave Classico, fennel seeds,
parsley, tomato & soft polenta

Primi

Taglierini – with English asparagus, herbs & aged parmesan
Linguine – with prosciutto di San Daniele, spring peas, mint & butter

Secondi

Capesante ai ferri – chargrilled Scottish scallops with salted anchovy, chilli
and grilled English asparagus
Branzino al forno – wild Sea Bass roasted with wild oregano, olives & lemon, with Tuscan
roast potatoes and trompette squash
Fegato di Vitello in padella – Calf's Liver seared with lemon zest, marjoram and capers,
with braised Italian spinach
Coscia d'Agnello – chargrilled marinated leg of lamb with salsa rossa piccante, wood-roasted
Violetta aubergine & baked fresh borlotti

Dolci

Affogato with Espresso   Chocolate Nemesis   Lemon Tart

Ed Ruscha

Bruschetta with Mozzarella and Spinach

Serves 2

7 ounces (200g) washed spinach leaves

1 large ball mozzarella, about 9 ounces (250g)

2 slices sourdough bread

1 garlic clove, peeled

2 ripe tomatoes, cut in half

7 fluid ounces (200ml) extra virgin olive oil

1 ounce (28g) picked mixed fresh summer herb leaves, to include marjoram and basil

1–2 olives, optional

In our private dining room at The River Cafe, we put antipasti on large plates to pass around the table. Put the bruschetta on one plate, with others for spinach, tomatoes and mozzarella, or other seasonal vegetables.

Blanch the spinach in a pot of boiling water for about 1 minute or until wilted. Drain well, pressing out excess water.

Tear the mozzarella onto two plates.

Grill the bread over charcoal or on a char-grill/griddle pan until nicely browned on both sides. Remove from the grill and rub generously with the garlic clove.

Squash the tomatoes onto the bruschetta (discard the tomato skin), then season well with sea salt and black pepper. Drizzle with olive oil. Put the bruschetta on the plates.

In a bowl, season the drained spinach. Toss with ¼–½ cup (50–100ml) extra virgin olive oil.

Arrange the spinach on the plates alongside the mozzarella and bruschetta. Drizzle with any remaining olive oil and add the herbs—plus an olive or two if you have them.

White Asparagus with Bottarga Butter

Serves 4

32 white asparagus spears

3½ ounces (100g) Sardinian bottarga from grey mullet roe

9 ounces (250g) unsalted butter, softened

juice of 1 lemon

We love the contrast between the delicate taste of the asparagus and the rich salty bottarga. Unlike with green asparagus, you need to be ruthless when peeling the stalks of white ones.

Snap the tough ends from the asparagus spears. Peel the stalks (up to the tips) using a potato peeler.

Grate about three-quarters of the bottarga stick on the finest holes of a cheese grater (reserve the remainder of the bottarga stick for adding at the end).

Beat the softened butter with the grated bottarga. Add the lemon juice and black pepper to taste. Check for seasoning and add a little sea salt, if required.

Bring a large pot of salted water to the boil. Add the asparagus and simmer for about 4 minutes, depending on the thickness of the spears, or until a knife tip can gently pierce the stalk. Drain the asparagus and arrange on four warm plates.

Put a dessertspoonful of the bottarga butter on top of each serving of warm asparagus. Grate the remaining bottarga over the plates and season with a little more black pepper. Serve immediately.

Raw Porcini Salad

Serves 4

4 large firm and fresh porcini

7 tablespoons (100ml) extra virgin olive oil, plus extra to drizzle

juice of ½ lemon

7 ounces (200g) arugula leaves

6 branches of fresh thyme leaves

This is a simple recipe we make only with very fresh porcini. The mushrooms should be pristine with wide, white stalks and brown, unbroken caps. If the undersides of the caps are yellowish brown it means the mushrooms are overripe. Never wash porcini.

Keeping the porcini whole, wipe the caps with a damp cloth and peel the stems, cutting off the base. Slice the porcini thinly lengthwise.

Combine the extra virgin olive oil and lemon juice with some sea salt and black pepper.

Wash and dry the arugula. Toss with the dressing and divide among four plates. Put the porcini on top. Season and sprinkle with the thyme leaves. Drizzle with extra virgin olive oil and serve.

Agretti with Tomato and Pangrattato

Serves 6–8

21 ounces (600g) agretti

1 stale ciabatta loaf

olive oil

½ recipe of Slow-cooked Tomato Sauce (see page 121)

When we first discovered agretti, it was impossible to source, but today it is available and worth searching for. Its dark grassy taste is brilliant with a rich slow-cooked tomato sauce, salty bottarga or with just olive oil, salt and pepper.

Snap off the bottom stalks from the agretti, just below the long leafy tops.

Pulse-chop the ciabatta into bread crumbs in a food processor. Heat some olive oil in a frying pan and toast the bread crumbs until they are golden. Lift out with a slotted spoon and drain well on paper towels.

Warm the tomato sauce.

Blanch the agretti in a pot of rapidly boiling salted water for 3 minutes or until tender. Drain and dry on paper towels to remove all the excess water.

Put the agretti on a plate and spoon the tomato sauce over it. Sprinkle with the bread crumbs and serve.

Zucchini Trifolati

Serves 6

12 small zucchini, trimmed

3 tablespoons olive oil

2 garlic cloves, peeled and sliced

½ cup (125ml) boiling water

a handful of fresh mint or basil leaves, roughly chopped

prosciutto di Parma or mozzarella, for serving

In the River Cafe kitchen, we all have our way of cooking this—some like the zucchini with more color, others paler—but we all agree that the most important thing is that all the water is absorbed into the zucchini.

Cut each zucchini at an angle into 3–4 slices.

Heat the olive oil in a large skillet, add the garlic and then the zucchini, and cook slowly for 15–20 minutes. When brown on all sides, add the boiling water and stir, scraping up the mixture that will have formed on the bottom of the pan. Cook until all the water has been absorbed and the zucchini are soft.

Add the mint or basil, season with sea salt and black pepper, and serve with prosciutto di Parma or mozzarella.

Fig and Cannellini Salad

Serves 6

12 ripe figs (black or green)

7 fluid ounces (200ml) extra virgin olive oil

1 bunch of fresh green basil

1 bunch of fresh purple basil

1 bunch of fresh mint

a selection of soft summer salad leaves, including arugula (about 3½ ounces [100g] per person)

10 ounces (300g) cooked cannellini beans (see page 256), kept in their cooking liquid

juice of 2 lemons

We often serve this with prosciutto di Parma.

Slice the figs and spread out on a large plate. Season with sea salt and black pepper and half of the extra virgin olive oil.

Pick the herbs and gently wash with the salad leaves. Spin dry and put aside.

Warm the cannellini beans in their cooking liquid, then drain and season.

In a large bowl, combine the seasoned figs and warm cannellini, stirring well. Gently toss through the salad and herb leaves. Season with the lemon juice, remaining extra virgin olive oil, sea salt and black pepper.

Put onto individual plates to serve.

Chickpea and Fennel Farinata

Serves 6–8

4¼ cups (about 1 liter) warm water

1¼ cups (300g) Italian chickpea flour

7 tablespoons (100ml) extra virgin olive oil, plus extra for the pan

1 teaspoon sea salt

2 tablespoons fennel seeds, or chopped fresh sage or rosemary leaves

Farinata is the street food of the coastal area of Liguria. We used to think it was only possible to make in a wood-burning oven, but discovered it comes out perfectly in our ovens at home.

Put the water in a large bowl and sift the flour into it. Whisk to combine, then add the extra virgin olive oil and salt. Cover and leave in a warm place for at least 2 hours, or overnight in the fridge.

Preheat the oven to 500°F (250°C).

Skim the foam from the top of the batter. Pour enough olive oil into a farinata pan or cast-iron skillet to generously coat the bottom. Pour in the batter (it should be about ¾ inch [1–2cm] deep). Top with the fennel seeds or herbs and some black pepper and stir a little.

Bake for 20–30 minutes or until the surface has bubbled and become crisp.

Panzanella

Serves 6

3½ ounces (100g)
salted capers

3½ ounces (100g)
salted anchovies

2 stale ciabatta loaves

2¼ pounds (1kg) fresh
plum tomatoes

1 garlic clove, peeled
and crushed to a paste
with a little sea salt

extra virgin olive oil

4 tablespoons red wine
vinegar

3 red bell peppers

3 yellow bell peppers

2 fresh red chiles

5 ounces (150g) black
olives, pitted

1 large bunch of fresh
basil leaves

Put the capers in a sieve and rinse under cold running water. Soak in cold water for 40 minutes, then rinse again.

Rinse the anchovies under cold running water to remove all the salt, then gently remove the spine bones and heads. Pat dry. Separate the anchovies into fillets.

Remove the crusts from the bread, cut the bread into thick slices and place in a large bowl.

Skin and quarter the tomatoes, remove the seeds into a sieve set over a bowl to retain the juices. Season with the garlic and black pepper, then add 1 cup (250ml) extra virgin olive oil and the red wine vinegar.

Pour the tomato juices over the bread and toss until the bread has absorbed the liquid. Depending on the staleness of the bread, more liquid may be required, in which case add a little more olive oil.

Heat the grill or a char-grill/griddle pan to high. Grill the whole peppers until blackened all over, then remove the skin and seeds (see Red and Yellow Peppers, Anchovies and Capers, page 64). Cut each pepper into eighths lengthwise. Grill the chiles until blackened, then skin, seed and chop finely.

In a large dish, make a layer of some of the bread. Top with some of all the other ingredients, then cover with another layer of bread. Continue until all the ingredients have been used. The final layer should have the peppers, tomatoes, capers, anchovies, olives and basil visible. Let it sit for an hour at room temperature. Drizzle with more extra virgin olive oil before serving.

The River Café

Rossini –
Prosecco
with fresh
strawberries £9

Thursday 8th September – Lunch

Antipasti

Fritto misto – deep fried zucchini, zucchini flowers, borage & sage £15
Calamari ai ferri – chargrilled squid with fresh red chilli & rocket £16
Mozzarella di Bufala – with Prosciutto, purple figs, mint & basil £15
Sarde al forno – butterflied sardines with pine nuts, warm borlotti beans,
raisins & fennel herb £13
Panzanella – Tuscan bread salad with tomato, yellow peppers,
basil, capers & anchovies £15
Mazzancolle cotte in Bianco – cold poached split Scottish langoustines
with basil mayonnaise £26
Carpaccio di Manzo – finely sliced beef fillet with thyme,
black pepper & mixed autumn leaves £17

Primi

Agnoli – fresh pasta stuffed with veal & prosciutto slow-cooked in
Soave Classico with sage butter & parmesan £15
Orrechiette – with raw plum tomatoes, basil & red wine vinegar £12
Taglierini alle Vongole – fine pasta with clams & pangratato, chilli & parsley £15
Tagliatelle con Funghi – hand-cut pasta with first of the season English porcini,
parsley & garlic £18

Secondi

Sogliola al forno – whole Dover sole wood-roasted with flowering marjoram
with zucchini & mint trifolati £33
Capesante in padella – Scottish scallops seared with aubergines, tomato, chilli, sage
& fresh cannellini beans £32
Salmone ai ferri – chargrilled wild Scottish salmon with Castelluccio lentils,
basil, mint, parsley & aioli £32
Coscia d'Agnello ai ferri – chargrilled marinated leg of lamb with potatoes 'Lucchese'
& salsa verde £32
Osso Bucco – veal shin slow-cooked with sage, thyme, tomato & Soave Classico with
swiss chard, girolles & gremolata £31
Gallo Cedrone al forno – first-of-the-season whole Yorkshire grouse stuffed with sage, wood
roasted on a Chianti Classico bruschetta £42

Susan Elias

Red and Yellow Peppers, Anchovies and Capers

Serves 6

2 ounces (50g) salted capers

3½ ounces (100g) salted anchovies

6 red bell peppers

6 yellow bell peppers

3 garlic cloves, peeled and cut into slivers

a handful of fresh basil leaves or picked marjoram

extra virgin olive oil

red wine vinegar (optional)

3 slices sourdough bread, cut in half

1 garlic clove, peeled and cut in half

Put the capers in a sieve and rinse under cold running water. Soak in cold water for 40 minutes, then rinse again.

Rinse the anchovies well under cold running water to remove all the salt, then gently remove the spine bones and heads. Pat dry and separate into fillets.

Heat the grill or a char-grill/griddle pan to high. Grill the whole peppers until blackened on all sides. Place in a plastic bag and seal. When cool, remove the blackened skin by rubbing the peppers in your hands or by scraping gently with a small knife on a board. Do not worry if they fall apart. Then remove the seeds and cores. Resist the temptation to clean the peppers under running water.

Layer the peppers in a large dish with slivers of garlic, capers, anchovies, basil or marjoram, black pepper and a generous amount of extra virgin olive oil. If you like, drizzle some red wine vinegar over the top. The final layer should have all the ingredients visible.

To make the bruschetta, toast the bread on both sides, then gently rub the garlic over one side only. Serve the peppers with the bruschetta.

Langoustines with Borlotti Beans

Serves 2

10 ounces (300g) podded fresh borlotti beans

2 garlic cloves, peeled

6 fresh sage leaves

¼ cup (50ml) olive oil

7 tablespoons (100ml) extra virgin olive oil, plus extra for drizzling

juice of 1 lemon

12 langoustines, cooked and peeled

1 fresh red chile, seeded and finely chopped

1 small bunch of fresh marjoram leaves, chopped

This is our favorite antipasto at Harry's Bar in Venice. The simple combination of creamy, fresh borlotti and delicate langoustines is perfection. Be generous with the olive oil you add at the end.

Put the borlotti beans in a large pot and cover with water. Add the garlic cloves, sage leaves and olive oil. Bring to the boil, then reduce the heat and simmer for about 40 minutes or until the beans are softened and edible.

Drain off any extra liquid from the pot. Add the extra virgin olive oil, lemon juice and peeled langoustines to the warm beans and toss gently over a low heat until the langoustines are just warmed through. Check the seasoning.

Transfer to serving plates, add the chile and marjoram, and drizzle with extra virgin olive oil.

Marinated Fresh Anchovies

Serves 6

2¼ pounds (1kg) fresh anchovies

2 teaspoons crumbled dried red chile

1 bunch of fresh flat-leaf parsley, finely chopped

juice of 2 lemons

1 cup (250ml) extra virgin olive oil

Fillet the anchovies by pulling the head and spine away from the fish, then cut off the tails and fins. You will have two fillets from each fish.

In a serving dish, arrange a layer of anchovies side by side, not overlapping. Sprinkle with a little sea salt, black pepper, chile and parsley. Add a generous amount of lemon juice and some extra virgin olive oil. Repeat the layers, making sure that the top layer is covered with oil and lemon.

Leave to marinate for about 2 hours before serving with either salad or bruschetta.

Jonas Wood

Primi

Zuppa

Zucchini Soup

Serves 6

2¼ pounds (1kg) medium zucchini, trimmed

2 tablespoons (25ml) olive oil

2 garlic cloves, peeled and chopped

2¼ cups (500ml) Chicken Stock (see page 156) or water

5 fluid ounces (140ml) heavy cream

1 small bunch of fresh basil leaves, chopped

1 small bunch of fresh mint leaves, chopped

4 ounces (120g) Parmesan, freshly grated

Like all of the soups in this chapter, this is a River Cafe classic—it is seasonal, easy to make, delicious to eat. In the photograph there are zucchini flowers. If you can buy them—or even better, grow them—they will add another dimension to the soup. But, as they are fragile, use them on the day you pick them.

Cut the zucchini lengthwise into quarters, then across into 1-inch (2.5cm) pieces. Heat the olive oil in a saucepan and cook the garlic and zucchini slowly for about 25 minutes or until the zucchini are very soft.

Add the stock and season with sea salt and black pepper, then simmer for another few minutes. Remove from the heat.

Put three-quarters of the zucchini in a food processor and purée. Return to the pan, and add the cream, basil, mint and Parmesan. Serve at room temperature.

Pappa al Pomodoro

Serves 10

9 pounds (4kg) ripe, sweet plum tomatoes

4 garlic cloves, peeled and cut into slivers

¾ cup (175ml) olive oil

1 stale sourdough loaf

1 large bunch of fresh basil leaves

extra virgin olive oil

This convinced Ruthie that the only food she wanted to cook was Italian. She was introduced to this recipe when she overheard, through a kitchen window, two sisters having a vehement argument about whether or not to add water to the tomatoes in a Pappa al Pomodoro. The sister who said "no" won the argument, but Ruthie then spotted the other one adding water when no one was looking.

Skin and seed the tomatoes, then chop them.

Put the garlic and olive oil into a pot and cook gently for a few minutes. Just before the garlic turns brown, add the tomatoes. Simmer for 30 minutes, stirring occasionally, until the tomatoes become concentrated. Season with sea salt and black pepper. Add 2½ cups (600ml) water and bring to the boil.

Cut most of the crust off the bread, then break or cut into large chunks. Put the bread into the tomato mixture and stir until the bread absorbs the liquid, adding more boiling water if the soup is too thick. Remove from the heat and allow to cool slightly.

If the basil leaves are large, tear into pieces. Stir the basil into the soup with ½–¾ cup (120–175ml) extra virgin olive oil. Let sit to allow the bread to absorb the flavor of the basil and oil. Add more extra virgin olive oil to each bowl when serving.

Summer Minestrone

Serves 10

2¼ pounds (1kg) thin asparagus

3⅓ pounds (1.5kg) fresh peas in their pods

4½ pounds (2kg) fresh, young fava beans in their pods

2 garlic cloves, peeled and chopped

1 small head celery, chopped

3 small red onions, peeled and chopped

4 tablespoons (60ml) olive oil

1 pound (450g) young green beans, trimmed and chopped

about 4¼ cups (1 liter) Chicken Stock (see page 156)

½ bunch of fresh basil leaves, finely chopped (or marjoram or mint)

1¼ cups (300ml) heavy cream

5 ounces (150g) Parmesan, freshly grated

½ cup (120ml) Pesto
(see page 107)

Trim or snap off the tough ends from the asparagus spears, then cut the tips and tender parts into ½-inch (1cm) pieces. Shell the peas and fava beans.

In a saucepan, sauté the garlic, celery and onions gently in the olive oil until soft—about 10 minutes.

Divide the asparagus, peas, fava beans and green beans between two bowls. Add one bowlful to the onion mixture and cook, stirring to coat with oil, for 5 minutes. Season to taste with sea salt and black pepper. Cover with the chicken stock and bring to the boil. Simmer for 15 minutes.

Add the remaining vegetables and cook for a further 10 minutes.

Remove from the heat and add the basil and cream. Stir. Cool to room temperature, then serve with Parmesan and pesto.

Pasta e Fagioli

Serves 10

9 ounces (250g) dried borlotti beans

½ garlic bulb, cut horizontally

a handful of fresh sage leaves

4 tablespoons olive oil

3 medium red onions, peeled and finely chopped

1 head celery, including the leaves, chopped

4 garlic cloves, peeled and chopped

3 dried red chiles, crumbled

1 bunch of fresh rosemary leaves, finely chopped or pounded

7 ounces (200g) pancetta

7 ounces (200g) plum tomatoes

9 ounces (250g) penne rigate

extra virgin olive oil

freshly grated Parmesan

Soak the beans and cook with the halved garlic bulb and sage as described on page 256. Leave in the cooking water until ready to use.

In a large saucepan, heat the oil and sauté the onions and celery together over a medium heat until the onions are soft but not brown. Add the garlic, chiles, rosemary and pancetta and continue to sauté, stirring. The pancetta should become almost crisp. Add the tomatoes with their juices, breaking them up with a spoon, and continue to cook, reducing the liquid, for about 20 minutes.

Drain the beans, reserving the cooking water. Transfer half of the cooked beans, with a little of their cooking water, to a food processor and mix, then add to the base in the saucepan along with the remaining whole beans. Add a little more of the cooking liquid if the soup seems too thick.

In a separate pot, cook the penne in boiling salted water until just al dente. Drain and stir into the soup. Check for seasoning.

Serve with a generous helping of new season's extra virgin olive oil and grated Parmesan.

Cannellini Bean Soup

Serves 6

9 ounces (250g) dried cannellini beans

½ garlic bulb, cut horizontally

a handful of fresh sage leaves

2–3 garlic cloves, peeled and chopped

3 tablespoons olive oil

1 bunch of fresh flat-leaf parsley leaves, chopped

extra virgin olive oil, to serve

The simplest of soups, but attention to detail is essential—the best cannellini and strong extra virgin olive oil will make all the difference.

Soak the beans and cook with the halved garlic bulb and sage as described on page 256. Drain, reserving the liquid.

In a large saucepan, cook the garlic in the olive oil until soft but not brown. Add the parsley and cook for a second, then add the beans and stir.

Put three-quarters of the bean mixture into a food processor with some of the reserved cooking liquid. Pulse briefly—you do not want a purée. Add more of the cooking liquid if necessary, but the soup should be thick.

Return to the saucepan and season with sea salt and black pepper. Reheat. If too thick, add more cooking liquid. Serve with a generous amount of extra virgin olive oil.

Ribollita

Serves 10

1 large bunch of fresh flat-leaf parsley, chopped

4 garlic cloves, peeled and chopped

2 whole heads celery, chopped

5 ounces (150g) carrots, peeled and chopped

2 medium red onions, peeled and chopped

4 tablespoons olive oil

9 ounces (250g) peeled plum tomatoes from a jar, drained of their juices

1 pound (500g) cavolo nero (Tuscan kale), stalks removed, leaves coarsely chopped

1 pound (500g) cooked cannellini or borlotti beans (see page 256), kept in their cooking liquid

1 large, stale ciabatta loaf, crusts removed, sliced or torn

extra virgin olive oil

Ribollita makes winter that little bit more bearable. It is a personal affair—as you can see from Rose's notes from a Tuscan cook—and you can add a variety of vegetables. But after years of making this soup, we like it best simply with cavolo nero (Tuscan kale), tomatoes, beans and bread.

In a large saucepan, sauté the parsley, garlic, celery, carrots and onions in the olive oil for about 30 minutes. Add the tomatoes and continue to cook on a gentle heat for a further 30 minutes. Stir from time to time.

Add the cavolo nero (Tuscan kale) and half of the cannellini or borlotti beans with enough of their cooking liquid to cover. Simmer for 30 minutes.

Drain the remaining beans. Purée them in a food processor, then add to the soup with just enough boiling water to make the soup liquid. Add the bread and a generous amount of extra virgin olive oil. Season with sea salt and black pepper. As exact amounts are not possible, you must balance the amount of liquid to bread so that the soup is very thick.

Chef River Café

Ribollita — celery, green beans, red onions, white
canelli beans (soaked overnight then
boiled gently, no salt for 2 hrs). Kale
black cabbage, spinach, Swiss chard
chopped fine all chopable
ingredients. Shred leaves - bread.
Fry celery beans onions etc in
good olive oil — Add shredded
veg + cooked canelli beans.
2 tins of plum tomatoes —
cook 1½. Add torn up bread
cook further ¾ hour. leave
to cool add ex virgin olive oil
fresh basil etc.

12½% SERVICE CHARGE + VAT INCLUDED
VAT REG No. 495 1252 37

THAMES WHARF RAINVILLE ROAD
LONDON W6 9HA 071-381 8824

Rose's notes on this recipe, 1989

Pumpkin Soup

Serves 6

3 tablespoons extra virgin olive oil, plus extra for the crostini and for serving

¼ cup (50g) unsalted butter

2 garlic cloves, peeled and finely chopped

1 small bunch of fresh marjoram leaves

3⅓ pounds (1.5kg) pumpkin, peeled, seeded and diced

½ pound (200g) new potatoes, peeled and cubed

2 dried red chiles, crumbled

4¼ cups (1 liter) Chicken Stock (see page 156)

6 slices ciabatta bread

1 garlic clove, peeled and halved

freshly grated Parmesan

Heat the extra virgin olive oil and butter in a saucepan and gently sauté the chopped garlic with the marjoram leaves until soft. Add the pumpkin and potatoes, and continue to cook for a minute. Add the chiles and season well with sea salt and black pepper. Pour in enough stock just to cover the pumpkin. Bring to the boil, then turn down the heat and simmer for 20–25 minutes or until the pumpkin is tender, adding more stock if necessary to keep the pumpkin covered.

Strain about a third of the stock from the pumpkin and set aside. Pour the contents of the pan into a food processor and pulse: the mixture should be very thick. Return to the saucepan and add the strained-off stock plus any remaining stock. Check for seasoning. The soup will be very thick. Reheat gently for serving.

For the crostini, toast the slices of ciabatta, then rub with the garlic halves and drizzle with extra virgin olive oil.

Serve the soup with Parmesan, extra virgin olive oil and the crostini.

The addition of ½ pound (200g) of cannellini beans is a variation of this soup—if you make this, omit the ciabatta crostini.

Pasta

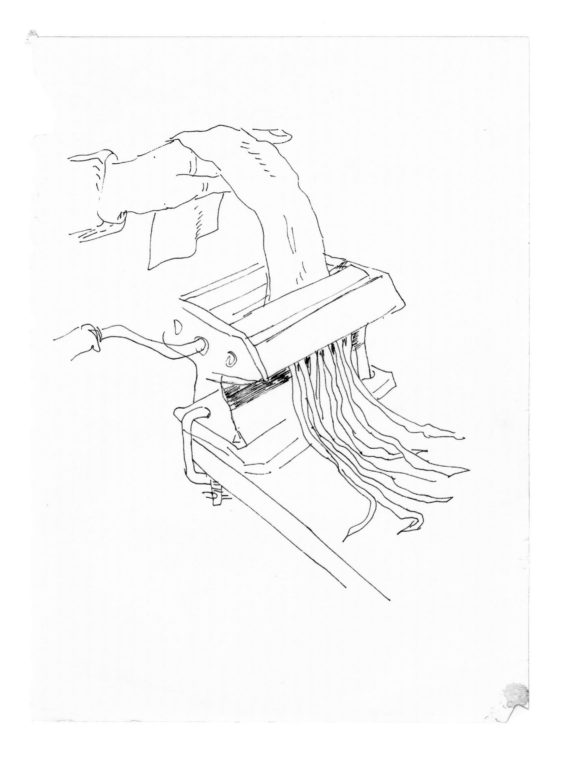

These drawings are by Rose.
She drew them when she
was living in Lucca, Italy,
with her family.

Fresh Pasta

Makes approximately 2¼ pounds (1kg)

3 cups (700g) Tipo 00 flour, plus extra for dusting

½ teaspoon sea salt

4 whole eggs (5 if they are small)

9 egg yolks (10 if the eggs are small)

semolina flour, for dusting

Put the flour and salt in a food processor and add the eggs and egg yolks. Pulse-blend until the ingredients start to come together into a loose ball of dough.

Lightly dust a flat surface with semolina and a little extra flour, then knead the pasta dough for about 3 minutes or until smooth. If the dough is very stiff and difficult to knead, you may have to put it back in the processor and blend in another whole egg.

Cut the dough into eight equal-sized pieces and briefly knead each into a ball. Wrap each ball in plastic wrap and allow to rest for at least 20 minutes, and up to 2 hours.

To prepare your dough for cutting into either tagliatelle or ravioli, put it through a pasta machine, following the manufacturer's instructions.

We put each ball through at the thickest setting ten times, folding the sheet into three each time to get a short thick strip, then turn it by a quarter and put it through the machine again. After ten such rolls and folds the pasta will feel silky. Only then do we reduce the machine setting gradually down to the thinness required. For tagliatelle, the setting is 2; for the rotolo, 1.5; for ravioli, a very thin setting of 0.5. These are the settings for our large commercial machine, but all machines are different.

If rolling by hand, you will have to hand-knead and hand-roll the dough the equivalent of ten times through the machine. This needs to be done in a cool place so that the pasta does not dry out.

Ravioli with Ricotta, Raw Tomato and Basil

Serves 10

27 ounces (750g) ricotta

freshly grated nutmeg

1 recipe Fresh Pasta (see page 94)

semolina flour, for dusting

5 very ripe, fresh San Marzano plum tomatoes

10 fresh basil leaves

extra virgin olive oil

salted ricotta

Make this in the summer when the tomatoes and basil are strong in flavor.

To make the filling, season the ricotta with sea salt, black pepper and nutmeg to taste, whisking with a fork. Set aside.

Divide the pasta dough into small amounts the size of a large egg and wrap them in plastic wrap (you will roll and fill them one at a time to prevent drying). Using a pasta machine, roll out one of the pieces of dough into a very thin, long strip (this is 1.5 thinness setting on our machine). Cut in half if too long.

Dust a large work surface with semolina flour and lay the sheet of pasta on this. Put teaspoons of filling about 2½ inches (6cm) apart on the sheet, placing them in the center of the half nearest to you so that you can fold the other half over. Brush the pasta around the filling with a pastry brush dipped in water—moisten enough so that the envelopes you are making will seal properly, but not so much that the pasta dough slides—then fold over.

Using a pasta cutter, make each raviolo by cutting on three sides (the fourth is the fold). Dust a large plate or tray with semolina flour and carefully place the ravioli on it, making sure they do not touch. Continue rolling, filling and folding the remaining pasta. You should have about fifty ravioli.

Cut the tomatoes in half, removing the core, and gently squeeze out the seeds. Chop the tomatoes finely and cut the basil leaves, then add with the tomatoes, season well and stir in a generous amount of extra virgin olive oil.

Bring a pot of salted water to the boil. You will need to cook the ravioli in batches. Put the ravioli into the boiling water, then lower the heat to a simmer: the ravioli will rise to the surface of the water after 30 seconds, but according to how thin you rolled the pasta, they will take up to 2 minutes to cook. Test on the join of the envelope where the pasta is thickest. Remove the ravioli with a draining spoon. Very gently warm the tomato sauce and serve over the ravioli on warm plates, with salted ricotta grated over.

Spaghetti with Lemon

Serves 6

½ pound (250g) spaghetti

juice of 3–4 lemons, preferably Amalfi lemons

⅔ cup (150ml) olive oil

5 ounces (140g) Parmesan, freshly grated

2 handfuls of fresh basil, leaves picked and finely chopped

finely grated lemon zest (optional)

Lemons, olive oil, basil . . . the only other ingredient needed is sun.

Cook the spaghetti in a generous amount of boiling salted water, then drain thoroughly and return to the pot.

Meanwhile, whisk the lemon juice with the olive oil, then stir in the Parmesan—it will melt into the mixture, making it thick and creamy. Season with sea salt and black pepper and add more lemon juice to taste.

Add the sauce to the spaghetti and shake the pot so that each strand of pasta is coated with the cheese. Finally, stir in the chopped basil and, ideally, some grated lemon zest.

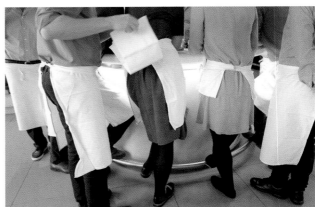

Linguine with Fresh and Dried Oregano

Serves 6

2 large handfuls of fresh oregano, very finely chopped

5 teaspoons (25g) dried oregano (on the branch), leaves crumbled

12 red cherry tomatoes, quartered and seeded

12 yellow cherry tomatoes, quartered and seeded

7 tablespoons (100ml) extra virgin olive oil

1 tablespoon red wine vinegar

½ pound (250g) linguine

The red wine vinegar lifts this recipe. It's important you serve this on hot plates.

Mix the fresh and dried oregano together.

Combine the tomatoes with the extra virgin olive oil, the red wine vinegar and sea salt and black pepper, then set aside to marinate.

Cook the linguine in a generous amount of boiling salted water, then drain and return to the pot. Toss with the oregano mixture and the marinated tomatoes until very hot, then serve.

Penne with Zucchini and Lemon Zest

Serves 6

14 medium zucchini (yellow, green or ridged varieties)

2 tablespoons olive oil

9 ounces (250g) unsalted butter

2 garlic cloves, peeled and thinly sliced

12 ounces (360g) penne

1 bunch of fresh mint leaves

2 lemons

9 ounces (250g) Parmesan (optional)

Trim the zucchini and chop into ½-inch (1cm) pieces.

Heat the olive oil with 7 tablespoons (100g) of the butter in a large saucepan. Add the zucchini and stir to coat with the butter and oil. Season with sea salt and black pepper and add the garlic slices. Allow to cook gently for about 20 minutes, stirring from time to time. The zucchini should mash up and become a mushy purée consistency.

Meanwhile, bring a pot of salted water to the boil.

Add the penne to the boiling water and cook for about 10 minutes or until al dente. Drain and add to the zucchini sauce. Add the remaining butter and the ripped-up mint leaves. Mix thoroughly.

Transfer to the serving plates and grate lemon zest on top. Add Parmesan shavings if you like.

Trofie with Pesto

Serves 6

7 ounces (200g) fresh basil leaves

7 ounces (200g) Parmesan, freshly grated, plus extra to serve

½ garlic clove, peeled

⅓ cup (75g) pine nuts

7 fluid ounces (200ml) extra virgin olive oil

18 ounces (500g) trofie pasta

For the pesto, put the basil leaves, Parmesan, garlic and pine nuts into a food processor fitted with a sharp blade. Add the extra virgin olive oil and some sea salt and black pepper, and blitz together to make a smooth paste.

Bring a large pot of salted water to the boil and cook the trofie for about 12 minutes. Drain the pasta and return to the pot.

Gently stir in the pesto. Check the seasoning and serve with grated Parmesan.

Tagliarini with Asparagus and Herbs

Serves 6

1½ pounds (675g) thin asparagus spears

4 garlic cloves, peeled

4 tablespoons chopped mixed fresh herbs (basil, mint, parsley, oregano)

7 tablespoons (100ml) heavy cream

2 tablespoons olive oil

¼ cup (50g) unsalted butter

9 ounces (250g) tagliarini or tagliatelle

4 ounces (120g) Parmesan, freshly grated

Trim or snap off the tough ends from the asparagus spears. Finely chop the asparagus all together with one of the garlic cloves and the herbs.

Bring the cream to the boil in a saucepan with the rest of the whole garlic cloves and simmer until the cloves are soft. Remove from the heat; discard the garlic.

Heat the olive oil and butter in a separate large saucepan and sauté half of the chopped asparagus for 5 minutes, stirring. Add the rest of the chopped asparagus followed by the flavored cream. Bring to the boil, then reduce the heat and simmer until the cream begins to thicken—about 6 minutes. Season. Remove from the heat and keep warm.

Cook the pasta in a generous amount of boiling salted water, then drain thoroughly. Add to the sauce along with about half of the Parmesan and toss together. Serve with the remaining Parmesan.

Tagliarini with Trevise

Serves 6

9 ounces (250g) trevise or red radicchio

6 ounces (175g) pancetta, cut into matchsticks

2 tablespoons olive oil

¼ cup (50g) unsalted butter

2 small red onions, peeled and sliced

2 tablespoons fresh thyme leaves

2 small garlic cloves, peeled and sliced

2 small dried red chiles, crumbled

9 ounces (250g) chicory, trimmed and sliced

2½ fluid ounces (75ml) white wine

5 fluid ounces (150ml) Chicken Stock (see page 156)

4 ounces (120g) Parmesan, freshly grated

9 ounces (250g) tagliarini

Trim the trevise or radicchio of its outer leaves and finely slice.

In a large saucepan, gently sauté the pancetta in half of the olive oil and all the butter until the pancetta releases its fat and begins to color—about 5 minutes. Add the onions and thyme and sauté for 5 minutes or until the onions are soft.

Add the garlic, chiles and the remaining olive oil and stir for a minute or two to combine before adding the trevise or radicchio and the chicory. Stir for a few minutes until the color changes and the trevise wilts.

Pour in the white wine and stock and bring to the boil. Simmer very gently for 20 minutes to reduce the liquid and thicken. Finally, stir in half of the Parmesan.

Cook the pasta in a generous amount of boiling salted water, then drain thoroughly. Stir into the sauce and season well. Serve with Parmesan.

The River Café

Rossini –
Prosecco with fresh
White Peach £9

Tuesday 7th July
Antipasti
Prosciutto di Parma — with Charentais melon
Mozzarella di Bufala — with Caponata Siciliana
Seppia con Inzimino — slow-cooked Cuttlefish zimino of chickpeas, tomato & swiss chard
Insalata — River Café garden ... peas & ba... tradizionale

Risotto di Piselli — with p... ricotta & lemon z...
Tagliatelle con Asparagi — ... and parmesan fondu...
Pappardelle — hand cut pasta w... ...lia Romagna

San Pietro al forno — wood-roasted ... cooked in Allegrin...
Salmone al sale — wild scottish salmon baked ... ...hard, datterini ...atoes ... at room tem...
Coscia d'Agnello ai ferri — chargrilled marinated leg of lamb with ...anfotta of ...bergine, potato, tomato, peppers and marjoram
Piccione ai ferri — chargrilled 1/2 Anjou Pigeon marinated in Valpolicella with green and yellow beans, speck and olives
Dolci
Affogato with Espresso   Lemon Tart   Hazelnut Ice Cream

PD 2017

Peter Doig

Spaghetti with Bottarga

Serves 6

9 ounces (250g) spaghetti or linguine

3 tablespoons olive oil

2 garlic cloves, peeled and finely chopped

¼ cup (50g) fresh flat-leaf parsley, very finely chopped

1 dried red chile, crumbled

3½ ounces (100g) bottarga, coarsely grated

juice of 1 lemon

Cook the pasta in a generous amount of boiling salted water, then drain thoroughly and return to the pot.

Meanwhile, heat the olive oil in a saucepan and sauté the garlic with the parsley and chile for a few seconds.

Add to the drained pasta, then stir in most of the bottarga.

Serve immediately with the remaining bottarga on top, plus a squeeze of lemon.

Rotolo di Spinaci

Serves 4–6

2 ounces (65g) dried porcini

2 pounds (800g) fresh spinach leaves

⅛ cup (20g) unsalted butter

¼ medium red onion, peeled and finely chopped

a handful of fresh marjoram leaves

1½ tablespoons olive oil

2 garlic cloves, peeled and finely chopped

about ¾ pound (350g) fresh ricotta

2 ounces (65g) Parmesan, freshly grated

freshly grated nutmeg

½ recipe Fresh Pasta (see page 94)

semolina flour, for dusting

extra freshly grated
Parmesan

Sage Butter
(see page 137)

To make the filling, first rehydrate the porcini by soaking them in warm to hot water for 15–20 minutes.

Blanch the spinach in boiling water until wilted. Drain and squeeze dry, then chop.

Heat the butter in a skillet and sauté the onion until soft. Add the marjoram and spinach, and stir to combine the flavors. Season, then cool.

Drain the porcini, reserving the soaking liquid (pass this through fine muslin or a filter to get rid of any grit). Heat the olive oil in a skillet and sauté the garlic gently for 30 seconds. Add the porcini and continue to sauté very gently for 10 minutes, adding a little of the porcini liquid from time to time to keep the mushrooms moist, not wet. Season and leave to cool. When cold, chop roughly.

Put the ricotta in a large bowl and mix lightly with a fork to break it up, then add the spinach mixture, Parmesan and a generous amount of nutmeg. Add sea salt and black pepper if necessary. Set aside.

Dust a large work surface with semolina flour and roll out the pasta dough by hand to a large sheet, as thin as possible; it does not matter if there are a few holes or tears. Cut the edges to straighten. You should have a piece of about 12 inches (30cm) square.

If you have a pasta machine, divide the dough in half and roll out into two very thin strips (this is 1.5 thinness setting on our machine). Join the strips to make a square, brushing the edges with water to seal.

Spoon the porcini along the edge of the pasta nearest to you, in a line about 1¼ inches (3cm) wide. Cover the rest of the pasta sheet with the spinach and ricotta mixture to a thickness of ½ inch (1cm). Now, starting at the mushroom edge, gently roll up the pasta sheet away from you into a large sausage shape.

Place the pasta roll on a clean towel and wrap in the towel—not too tightly as the pasta will expand a little during cooking. Secure with string to hold the roll in shape, tying at either end like a Christmas cracker and also in the middle.

Fill a fish poacher with water and bring to the boil. Add sea salt and the pasta roll, then cover and simmer for 13–18 minutes, according to the thickness of the roll—we usually make rolls of 3-inch (7cm) diameter.

Unwrap the pasta roll and place it on a board. Cut across into ½-inch (1cm) slices. Serve 4–6 slices per person, with extra grated Parmesan and some sage butter.

Quick Sweet Tomato Sauce

Serves 6–8

3 tablespoons olive oil

3 garlic cloves, peeled and cut into slivers

two 36-ounce (1kg) jars peeled plum tomatoes, drained of their juices

a handful of fresh basil or oregano leaves

Heat 1–2 tablespoons of the olive oil in a large pan and sauté the garlic until it is soft but not brown. Add the tomatoes with some sea salt and black pepper and cook fiercely, stirring constantly to prevent the tomatoes from sticking as they break up. As they cook, the tomatoes will release their juices. When this liquid has evaporated, add the remaining olive oil, the basil or oregano, and more seasoning if necessary. Serve hot.

Slow-cooked Tomato Sauce

Serves 6–8

3 tablespoons olive oil

2 medium red onions, peeled and sliced as thinly as possible into rounds

2 garlic cloves, peeled and cut into slivers

two 36-ounce (1kg) jars peeled plum tomatoes, drained of their juices

Heat the olive oil in a large saucepan or frying pan, add the onions and cook over a low heat until they are very soft. This will take at least 40 minutes—the onions must eventually disappear into the tomato sauce. Some 5 minutes before the end of cooking, add the garlic.

Now add the tomatoes and stir to break them up. Season with sea salt and black pepper. Cook slowly, stirring occasionally, for at least 1½ hours. When the sauce is ready, it will be dark red and extremely thick, with no juice at all, and the oil will have come to the surface. Serve hot.

Penne with Cloe's Quick Sausage Sauce

Serves 6

2 tablespoons olive oil

2 small red onions, peeled and chopped

5 fresh Italian spiced pork sausages, meat removed from skins and crumbled

2 tablespoons chopped fresh rosemary leaves

2 bay leaves

2 small dried red chiles, crumbled

36-ounce (1kg) jar peeled plum tomatoes, drained and chopped

9 ounces (250g) penne rigate

5 fluid ounces (150ml) heavy cream

4 ounces (120g) Parmesan, freshly grated

Cloe Peploe and Adam Alvarez were two of Rose's closest friends and they often cooked together. Cloe and Adam disagreed about the way to make this sauce, so we put both versions in our first book and again, here, as a tribute to them both.

In a large saucepan, heat the olive oil and sauté the onions until light brown. Add the crumbled sausages, the rosemary, bay leaves and chiles. Sauté together over a high heat, stirring to mash the sausages.

Remove all but 1 tablespoon of the fat, then continue to cook for 20 minutes. The sausage meat should become brown and almost disintegrate. Add the tomatoes, stir and bring to the boil. Remove from the heat and season.

Cook the penne in a generous amount of boiling salted water, then drain.

Stir the cream into the sauce along with the drained penne and half of the Parmesan. Serve with the remaining Parmesan.

Penne with Adam's Slow-cooked Sausage Sauce

Serves 6

2 tablespoons olive oil

8 fresh Italian spiced pork sausages, meat removed from skins and crumbled

2 small red onions, peeled and chopped

2 garlic cloves, peeled and chopped

2 small dried red chiles, crumbled

2 bay leaves

1 cup (250ml) Chianti Classico

36-ounce (1kg) jar peeled plum tomatoes, drained of their juices

¼ nutmeg, freshly grated

4 ounces (120g) Parmesan, freshly grated

5 fluid ounces (150ml) heavy cream

9 ounces (250g) penne rigate

Heat the olive oil in a large skillet and sauté the sausage meat, stirring and breaking up the pieces. After the juices from the meat have evaporated and the fat begins to run, add the onions, garlic, chiles and bay leaves. Cook gently for about 30 minutes until the onions are brown.

Pour in the wine, increase the heat and cook until the wine evaporates. Now add the tomatoes. Lower the heat and simmer gently for 45–60 minutes or until you have a thick sauce. Season with the nutmeg and sea salt (and black pepper, if the sausages were not spicy). Stir in the Parmesan and cream.

Cook the penne in a generous amount of boiling salted water, then drain well. Add the penne to the sauce, combine and serve.

Orecchiette with Broccoli Rabe, Anchovy and Pangrattato

Serves 6

8 ounces (250g) sourdough bread

olive oil

4 garlic cloves,
peeled—
3 thinly sliced,
1 left whole

1⅓ pounds (600g)
broccoli rabe
(tender leaves
and stems only)

5 salted anchovies

a pinch of red
pepper flakes

a handful of fresh
flat-leaf parsley,
roughly chopped

9 ounces (500g)
orecchiette

For the pangrattato (bread crumbs), remove the crusts from the bread and chop in a food processor to form coarse crumbs.

Heat 2 tablespoons of olive oil in a saucepan with the whole garlic clove. When the garlic is golden, add the crumbs to the oil and toast until golden brown. Remove with a slotted spoon and spread out on paper towels to drain any excess oil. Season the crumbs with sea salt and black pepper while still warm.

Boil the broccoli rabe in salted water until tender—about 5 minutes. Drain and roughly chop.

Rinse the anchovies under cold running water to remove all the salt, then gently remove the spine bones and heads. Pat dry. Separate the anchovies into fillets.

Heat another 2 tablespoons of olive oil in a skillet. Add the thinly sliced garlic, red pepper flakes, black pepper and just a pinch of sea salt (the anchovies will add further seasoning) and turn on a medium heat. When the garlic starts to turn golden, add the anchovy fillets. Continue to sauté until the anchovies disintegrate. Add the parsley.

Add the (still slightly wet) broccoli rabe and increase the heat so that the whole mixture bubbles furiously for a minute. Keep tossing the greens until completely coated. Reduce the heat and simmer briefly, but not too long or the bright green color will become dull. Check the seasoning.

Cook the orecchiette in a generous amount of boiling salted water.
Drain and toss through the broccoli rabe sauce. Sprinkle with the pangrattato.

Rigatoni with Cavolo Nero and New Olive Oil

Serves 6

2¼ pounds (1kg) cavolo nero (Tuscan kale) leaves

2 garlic cloves, peeled

1 cup (250ml) extra virgin olive oil

9 ounces (500g) rigatoni

freshly grated Parmesan

This pasta is the celebration of two ingredients that arrive at the same moment in the year—cavolo nero (Tuscan kale) and the first pressed, peppery extra virgin olive oil. When we started The River Cafe in 1987, cavolo nero was nowhere to be found, so we brought the seeds back from Italy. Now you can find it everywhere— but only buy it after the first frost, and not after the winter months.

Remove the stalks from the cavolo nero leaves, but keep the leaves whole. Blanch them in a generous amount of boiling salted water along with the garlic cloves for 5 minutes. Drain. Put the blanched cavolo nero and garlic into a food processor and pulse-chop to a purée. In the last couple of seconds of blending, pour in about 7 fluid ounces (200ml) of the extra virgin olive oil. This will make a fairly liquid, dark green purée. Season well.

Cook the rigatoni in a generous amount of boiling salted water, then drain thoroughly. Put the pasta into a bowl, add the sauce and stir until each piece is thickly coated. Pour over the remaining extra virgin olive oil and serve with Parmesan.

Linguine with Crab

Serves 10

2 large live male crabs, about 4½–6¾ pounds (2–3kg) total weight

3 fresh red chiles, seeded and finely chopped

3 handfuls of fresh flat-leaf parsley, finely chopped

juice of 4 lemons

3 garlic cloves, peeled and ground to a paste with a little sea salt

1 cup (250ml) olive oil

9 ounces (500g) linguine

extra virgin olive oil

Ask the fishmonger to kill the crabs for you.

In a pot large enough to hold both crabs, bring enough water to the boil to cover them. Add the crabs and boil gently for 20 minutes. Remove the crabs from the water and leave to cool.

Remove the claws and legs. Break the bodies open carefully. Remove the brown meat from inside the shell and transfer, along with any juices, to a large bowl. Remove the white meat from the claws and legs and add to the brown meat in the bowl. Mix together.

Add the chiles, most of the chopped parsley, the lemon juice and garlic to the crab mixture. Season well. Stir in the olive oil. This sauce should be quite liquid.

Cook the linguine in a generous amount of boiling salted water, then drain thoroughly. Stir into the crab sauce, but do not reheat. Serve sprinkled with the remaining chopped parsley and a generous amount of extra virgin olive oil.

Mezze Paccheri, Black Pepper and Langoustine

Serves 6

1¼ pounds (600g) mezze paccheri

¼ cup (60g) unsalted butter

5 ounces (150g) Pecorino, freshly grated, plus extra for grating on top

¾ pound (360g) medium langoustines (4–5 langoustines per person), cooked and peeled

about 4 teaspoons (20g) coarsely ground black pepper

In a world of rules, including the seminal one that you must never put cheese on a fish pasta, this eccentric recipe combining Pecorino and langoustines commits the cardinal sin. It is incredibly delicious and proves that rules are made to be broken.

Cook the mezze paccheri pasta in plenty of boiling salted water until al dente. When draining the pasta, reserve some of the cooking water for the sauce.

Melt the butter with the Pecorino in a separate large pan over a low heat, using some of the reserved pasta water to create a sauce.

Cut the langoustines into pieces and add to the Pecorino sauce with black pepper to taste. Add the hot cooked pasta and mix until you have a glossy sauce coating the pasta, adding more reserved pasta water if needed.

Serve with extra Pecorino grated on top.

Spinach and Ricotta Gnocchi

Serves 6

2¼ pounds (1kg) fresh spinach

¼ cup (50g) unsalted butter

1 small bunch of fresh marjoram

14 ounces (400g) fresh ricotta

8 teaspoons (40g) all-purpose flour

3 egg yolks

¼ nutmeg, grated

4 ounces (120g) Parmesan, freshly grated, plus extra for serving

1 cup (225g) unsalted butter

1 bunch of fresh sage leaves

Blanch the spinach in boiling water until wilted, then squeeze dry. You should have about ¾ pound (350g) blanched spinach.

Melt the ¼ cup butter in a pan, add the picked marjoram leaves and cook for a minute. Add the spinach and stir to combine the flavors. Season, then leave to cool. When cooled, chop roughly.

In a large bowl, lightly beat the ricotta with a fork. Sift in the flour. Add the egg yolks, nutmeg and Parmesan and mix well. Finally, fold in the cooled spinach mixture until well combined. Taste for seasoning.

Line a baking sheet with parchment paper.

Use two dessertspoons for shaping the gnocchi: with one of them take a small spoonful of the mixture and, using the other spoon, mold the mixture so that it forms a gnoccho (a small oval dumpling about ¾ inch [2cm] in diameter). Place on the baking sheet. Continue making the gnocchi—they should all be the same size.

To make the sage butter, heat the 1 cup butter gently so it separates. Pour out the clarified butter into a clean pan and return to the heat. When very hot, add the sage leaves. Remove from the heat and allow to cool.

Bring a large pot of salted water to the boil, then lower the heat to a simmer. Gently place the gnocchi in the water in batches—it is important not to overcrowd the pot. When the gnocchi come back to the surface, remove carefully with a slotted spoon and briefly place the spoon on paper towels to drain off excess water.

Keep the gnocchi warm, tossed with some of the sage butter, in a warm oven while you cook the rest.

Serve immediately on warm plates with the remaining sage butter and extra Parmesan.

Risotto

Risotto with Amarone di Valpolicella

Serves 6

1¼ cups (300ml) Chicken Stock (see page 156)

⅔ cup (150g) unsalted butter, softened

1 medium red onion, peeled and chopped

1 head celery, washed and finely chopped

10 ounces (300g) risotto rice

1 bottle (750ml) Amarone di Valpolicella

5 ounces (150g) Parmesan, freshly grated

crème fraîche (optional)

Shocking as it seems, you do need a whole bottle of Amarone for this risotto. Don't make it with any less.

Heat the chicken stock and check for seasoning.

Melt two-thirds of the butter in a large saucepan and gently sauté the onion and celery for about 20 minutes or until light brown. Add the rice and stir to coat with butter.

Increase the heat and gradually pour in 2 cups (500ml) of the wine, slowly letting the wine be absorbed by the rice. Then add the hot stock, ladle by ladle, stirring all the time and only adding more stock when the rice has absorbed the previous addition.

When all the stock has been absorbed and the rice is almost cooked, gradually add the remaining wine, stirring. The rice will have taken on the color of the wine.

Add half of the Parmesan and the remaining butter and season, taking care not to overstir. Serve with the rest of the Parmesan and a dollop of crème fraîche on top, if using.

Risotto with Roast Partridge

Serves 6

3 prepared grey-legged partridges

¼ cup (50g) unsalted butter, softened

olive oil

7 ounces (200g) pancetta, cut into large dice

2 garlic cloves, peeled

Preheat the oven to 400°F (200°C).

1 bunch of fresh sage leaves

Smother the partridges with the ¼ cup (55g) butter and season inside and out.

7 fluid ounces (200ml) Chianti

In an ovenproof pan large enough to fit the birds side by side, gently heat some olive oil and sauté the pancetta, garlic and sage leaves until the pancetta is golden and the sage is crisp. Add the partridges, breast side up, and pour in half of the wine. Transfer to the hot oven and roast for 10 minutes.

4¼ cups (1 liter) Chicken Stock (see page 156)

½ cup (120g) unsalted butter, softened

Turn the birds over and add the rest of the wine. Return to the oven to roast for a further 5 minutes. Leave to rest in a warm place while preparing the risotto.

5 tablespoons olive oil

Heat the chicken stock.

1 medium red onion, peeled and finely chopped

1 celery heart, finely chopped

Melt 4 tablespoons (60g) of the butter with the olive oil in a large skillet and gently sauté the onion and celery for 15–20 minutes until soft. Add the rice and, off the heat, stir until the rice becomes totally coated—this takes only a minute.

10 ounces (300g) risotto rice

⅓ cup (75ml) extra dry white Vermouth

Return to a high heat, add the Vermouth and simmer, stirring constantly, until the rice has absorbed nearly all the liquid. Start adding the hot stock, ladle by ladle, adding more as each is absorbed and always stirring. After 15–20 minutes nearly all the stock will have been added and absorbed by the rice; each grain will have a creamy coating but will remain al dente. Check the seasoning.

6 ounces (175g) Parmesan, freshly grated

Add the remaining butter in small pieces and the Parmesan. Stir just to combine. Serve each person half a partridge, with its cooking juices, resting on the risotto.

Risotto with Porcini and Chanterelles

Serves 6

2¼ pounds (1kg) mixed fresh porcini and chanterelles

⅔ cup (150ml) extra virgin olive oil

1 garlic clove, peeled and finely chopped

1 teaspoon picked fresh thyme leaves

4¼ cups (1 liter) Chicken Stock (see page 156)

½ cup (100g) unsalted butter

1 medium red onion, peeled and finely chopped

10 ounces (300g) risotto rice

1 cup (250ml) extra dry white Vermouth

9 ounces (250g). Parmesan, freshly grated

1 bunch of fresh flat-leaf parsley leaves, finely chopped

Pick through the mushrooms, removing any leaves and the base of the stems. Clean the mushrooms by brushing them lightly with a dry pastry brush. Wipe clean the caps of the porcini. Tear any large mushrooms into smaller pieces.

In a frying pan, heat 3 tablespoons of the extra virgin olive oil. Add half of the mushrooms along with half of the chopped garlic and thyme. Season with sea salt and black pepper. Sauté for a couple of minutes until cooked and any liquid has evaporated.

Remove this batch of mushrooms from the pan and cook the remainder in the same way, with another 3 tablespoons of olive oil, the rest of the garlic and thyme, and seasoning.

Heat the chicken stock.

In a medium saucepan, heat half of the butter with the remaining olive oil. Add the chopped onion and cook on a gentle heat until the onion is soft.

Add the rice and stir until each grain is coated with the butter and oil. Pour in the Vermouth and cook until it has been absorbed, stirring all the while, then start adding the hot stock, ladle by ladle, constantly stirring, and allowing each ladleful to be absorbed by the rice before adding the next. Continue to cook in this way until the rice is al dente—this usually takes about 20 minutes.

Add the cooked wild mushrooms, the remaining butter, the Parmesan and chopped parsley. Serve immediately.

Risotto Nero with Swiss Chard

Serves 6

4¼ cups (1 liter) Fish Stock (see page 157)

1 large cuttlefish, cleaned by the fishmonger (ask for the ink sacs)

7 tablespoons (100ml) olive oil

1 medium red onion, peeled and finely chopped

2 garlic cloves, peeled and finely chopped

1 dried red chile, crumbled

10 ounces (300g) risotto rice

7 tablespoons (100ml) white wine

4 peeled plum tomatoes from a jar, drained of their juices

2 sachets squid ink (if you do not have the ink from the cuttlefish)

3 tablespoons chopped fresh flat-leaf parsley

7 ounces (200g) cooked Swiss chard, chopped

⅓ cup (75g) unsalted butter

Heat the fish stock.

Finely chop the cuttlefish. Choose a large pan and warm the olive oil in it, then sauté the onion and garlic until translucent. Add the cuttlefish (not the ink) and chile, and season with sea salt and black pepper. Stir to combine, then add the rice and sauté for 2–3 minutes or until opaque.

Add the wine and tomatoes and simmer until most of the liquid has been absorbed by the rice, stirring to prevent sticking. Now add the ink. When each grain of rice has become black, start to add the hot stock, a ladleful at a time, only adding more when the previous addition has been absorbed. Continue until the rice is cooked al dente.

Remove from the heat and stir in the parsley and Swiss chard. Check the seasoning. Add the butter and serve immediately.

The River Café

Rossini – £14
Prosecco with fresh
strawberries

Tuesday 2nd May – Set Lunch
Antipasti
Insalata di Piselli – spring pea salad with sweet & bitter leaves & balsamic
Vitello Tonnato – thinly sliced Veal with tuna mayonnaise, capers, anchovy & parsley
Mozzarella di Bufala – marinated in crème fraiche with spring herbs,
rainbow chard and chickpea farinata

Primi
Zuppa di Zucchini e Fiore di Zucchini
Pappardelle – hand-cut pasta with rabbit, pancetta, bay & pecorino
Rotolo di Spinaci – fresh pasta sheets rolled with Buffalo ricotta, spinach, porcini & sage
Risotto di Asparagi – with green & white asparagus, vermouth & parmesan

Secondi
Coda di Rospo al forno – Cornish Monkfish roasted in Pinot Bianco with anchovy & rosemary sauce
and warm agretti
San Pietro ai ferri – wood-roast John Dory fillet with capers, lemon & thyme, with Italian spinach
& artichoke 'alla Romana'
Stinco di Vitello – Veal shin slow-cooked in I Sistri Chardonnay with sage, spinach & gremolata
Coscia d'Agnello ai ferri – chargrilled marinated leg of Lamb with grilled whole red chilli,
smashed cannellini & braised cicoria

Dolci
Lemon Tart   Chocolate Nemesis   Roasted Almond Ice Cream

12 1/2% OPTIONAL SERVICE CHARGE WILL BE ADDED
IF YOU HAVE A FOOD ALLERGY, PLEASE SPEAK TO US BEFORE ORDERING

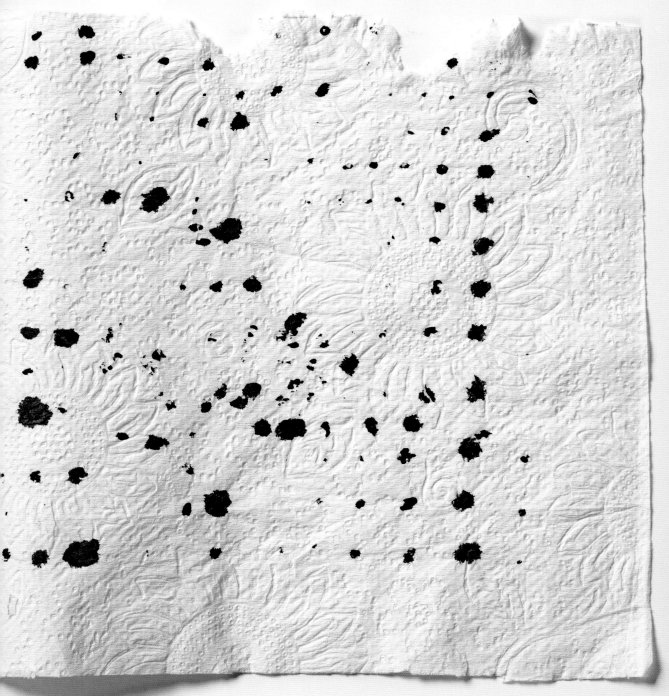

Brice Marden

Nettle Risotto with Taleggio

Serves 6

10 ounces (300g) nettles

⅞ cup (200g) unsalted butter

1 medium red onion, peeled and finely chopped

1 small head celery, trimmed and finely chopped

1 garlic clove, peeled and finely chopped

10 ounces (300g) risotto rice

7 fluid ounces (200ml) Soave Classico

3½ cups (750ml) warmed Chicken Stock (see page 156)

9 ounces (250g) Taleggio, skin removed, cut into ½-inch (1cm) cubes

Bring a pot of water to the boil and cook the nettles for about 4 minutes. Drain well and, using a food processor, pulse the nettles into a smooth paste.

In a large pan, melt half of the butter and gently sauté the onion, celery and garlic until translucent. Season with sea salt and black pepper.

Add the rice and sauté for about 5 minutes over a medium heat. Add the wine and allow it to bubble and become absorbed by the rice before beginning to add the stock. A ladleful at a time, gradually add the hot stock, stirring often until the stock is absorbed and the rice is cooked. This will take 15–20 minutes, cooking over a gentle heat.

When the rice is cooked, check for seasoning and stir in the nettle purée. Add the cubes of Taleggio and allow to melt in. Serve immediately.

Risotto with Zucchini Flowers

Serves 6

18 male zucchini flowers

6 small young zucchini, trimmed

4¼ cups (1 liter) Chicken Stock (see page 156)

⅔ cup (150g) unsalted butter, softened

2 tablespoons olive oil

1 medium red onion, peeled and very finely chopped

10 ounces (300g) risotto rice

⅓ cup (75ml) extra dry white Vermouth

6 ounces (175g) Parmesan, freshly grated

a handful of fresh basil leaves

Prepare the flowers by removing the stamens and spiky sepals. Tear each flower vertically into 4 strands. Brush to get rid of any dust or insects, but do not wash.

Slice the zucchini into very fine disks, as thin as the flower strands.

Heat the chicken stock and check for seasoning.

Melt half of the butter and all the olive oil in a large pan and gently sauté the onion for 15 minutes or until soft. Add the rice and stir until the grains are totally coated with butter—this only takes a minute. Add the Vermouth and stir until it has been absorbed. Add two or so ladlefuls of hot stock, or just enough to cover the rice, and simmer, stirring, until the rice has absorbed nearly all the liquid. Continue to add more stock as the previous addition is absorbed.

After about 20 minutes of cooking, add the zucchini and then the flower strands, along with the last two or three ladlefuls of stock. When the risotto is ready, the zucchini should still have a little bite; the flowers will have disappeared; and the rice will have a creamy coating but will remain al dente.

Add the remaining butter, in small pieces, the Parmesan and basil leaves, being careful not to overstir. Serve immediately.

Pumpkin Risotto

Serves 6

2 pounds (950g) deep yellow pumpkin or squash, whole or 1 large slice, with the skin

about 5 tablespoons olive oil

2 tablespoons fresh marjoram or oregano leaves

2 garlic cloves, peeled and thickly sliced

4¼ cups (1 liter) Chicken Stock (see page 156)

⅔ cup (150g) unsalted butter, softened

1 medium red onion, peeled and very finely chopped

10 ounces (300g) risotto rice

⅓ cup (75ml) extra dry white Vermouth

6 ounces (175g) Parmesan, freshly grated

Preheat the oven to 425°F (220°C).

Remove the seeds and fibers from the pumpkin or squash, cutting the flesh (with skin) into large chunks. Place, skin side down, on a baking sheet brushed with a little of the olive oil. Season with sea salt and black pepper and scatter the herbs and garlic over it. Drizzle with 3 tablespoons of the olive oil.

Cover with foil and bake the pumpkin for 50 minutes or until it is soft and shriveled and has begun to brown at the edges. Allow to cool, scraping the flesh from the skin, and reserve with the juices.

Heat the chicken stock and check for seasoning.

Melt half of the butter and the remaining olive oil in a large pan. Gently sauté the onion for 15 minutes or until soft. Add the rice and stir until the grains become coated with butter. Add the Vermouth and stir until it has been absorbed. Add two ladlefuls of hot stock, or just enough to cover the rice, and simmer, stirring, until the rice has absorbed nearly all the liquid. Continue to add more stock as the previous addition is absorbed.

After 15 minutes, nearly all the stock will have been absorbed by the rice; each grain will have a creamy coating, but will remain al dente.

Add the remaining butter, in small pieces, the pumpkin and Parmesan, being careful not to overstir. Serve immediately.

153

Chicken Stock

Makes about 8½ cups (2 liters)

2 chicken carcasses (roasted or raw), plus giblets

1 medium red onion, peeled and halved

2 medium carrots, peeled

4 celery stalks

2 garlic cloves, peeled

a few fresh flat-leaf parsley stalks

5 black peppercorns

3 bay leaves or 5 fresh thyme sprigs

sea salt

Put all the ingredients, except the sea salt, into a large stockpot and cover with about 8½ cups (2 liters) cold water. Bring to the boil, skimming off the scum as it comes to the surface. Lower the heat and simmer, uncovered, very gently for 1½ hours.

Strain, season with salt and leave to cool. If not using immediately, keep in the refrigerator for up to 2 days or freeze.

Fish Stock

Makes about 8½ cups (2 liters)

1¾–2¼ pounds (780g–1kg) white fish bones

2 medium red onions, peeled and cut into quarters from root to tip

2 medium carrots, peeled and sliced

4 celery stalks

a few fresh flat-leaf parsley stalks

6 white or black peppercorns

2 bay leaves

1 fennel bulb, untrimmed, cut in half vertically

Put all the ingredients into a large stockpot and cover with about 8½ cups (2 liters) cold water. Bring to the boil, skimming off the scum as it comes to the surface. Lower the heat and simmer, uncovered, gently for 15 minutes—in order to achieve a fresh-tasting stock, do not be tempted to simmer longer than this.

Strain and use immediately, or freeze.

Polenta

Polenta

Serves 6–8

12 ounces (350g) coarse polenta

1 teaspoon sea salt

⅔ cup (150g) unsalted butter, softened

7 ounces (200g) Parmesan, freshly grated

Put the polenta in a large spouted measuring cup so that it can be poured in a steady stream.

Bring 8 cups (1.75 liters) water to the boil in a large pot and add the salt. Lower the heat to a simmer and slowly add the polenta, stirring with a whisk until completely blended. It will now start to bubble volcanically.

Reduce the heat to as low as possible, cover with a lid and cook the polenta for 40–45 minutes, stirring from time to time with a wooden spoon to prevent a skin from forming on the top. The polenta is cooked when it falls away from the sides of the pan and has become very dense and thick.

Stir in the butter and Parmesan, and season generously with sea salt and black pepper.

Grilled Polenta

Make the polenta as described, omitting the butter and Parmesan. Transfer to a large, flat baking sheet or plate and spread out to form a cake about 1 inch (2.5cm) thick. Leave until completely cold, then cut into wedges or slices.

Heat the grill or a char-grill/griddle pan to very hot. Brush the pieces of polenta on both sides with olive oil and grill for 3 minutes per side or until crisp and brown.

To celebrate the opening of their new food hall in 1992,
Harvey Nichols asked The River Cafe and other restaurants
to create an art installation using one ingredient. We made
a "polenta mountain" in The River Cafe and Nigel Finch
directed a short film about the process.

PESCE

Grilled Squid, Fresh Red Chile and Arugula

Red Mullet with Capers and Clams

Sea Bass Baked in Salt

Poached Turbot Tranche

Dover Sole with Capers and Marjoram

Grilled Sea Bass Fillets

Squid with Anchovies and Peas

Roast Monkfish with Tomatoes and Oregano

Ligurian Fish Stew

Scallops with Sage and Capers

CARNE

Beef Fillet with Salmoriglio

Veal Shank Slow-cooked with Barolo and Sage

Sweetbread Fritto Misto

Marinated Grilled Lamb

Pan-fried Calf's Liver with Cavolo Nero

Pork Cooked in Milk

Braised Beef Fillet

Pork Braised with Vinegar

Bollito Misto

Pheasant with Josephine Dore

Roast Grouse with Pancetta

Roast Pigeon Stuffed with Cotechino

SALSA

Bagnet

Salsa Verde

Salmoriglio

Salsa di Dragoncello

Salsa di Peperoncini Scottati

Salsa di Peperoncini Rossi

Salsa Calda d'Acciughe

Salsa Fredda d'Acciughe

Salsa Pasta d'Olive

Salsa Rossa

Secondi

Grilled Squid, Fresh Red Chile and Arugula

Serves 4

8 medium squid (no bigger than your hand)

6 large, fresh red chiles, seeded and very finely chopped

⅔ cup (150ml) extra virgin olive oil

½ pound (225g) arugula

4 tablespoons oil
and lemon dressing
(see page 37)

1 lemon, cut into quarters

Grilled squid with fresh red chile and arugula has been on the menu every day since The River Cafe opened. With its primary colors and strong flavors the combination of just three ingredients is simple, pure and right.

Clean the squid by cutting the body open to make a flat piece and scraping out the guts. Keep the tentacles in their bunches but remove the eyes and mouth. Using a serrated knife, score the inner side of the flattened squid body with parallel lines ½ inch (1cm) apart, and then lines equally apart the other way to make crosshatching.

To make the sauce, put the chopped chiles in a bowl and cover with the extra virgin olive oil. Season with sea salt and black pepper.

Heat a charcoal fire in the barbecue or a char-grill/griddle pan until very hot. Place the squid (including the tentacles), scored side down, on the grill, season with sea salt and black pepper, and grill for 1–2 minutes. Turn the squid pieces over; they will immediately curl up, by which time they will be cooked.

Toss the arugula in the dressing. Arrange two squid bodies with tentacles on each plate with some of the arugula. Put a little of the chile sauce on the squid and serve with the lemon quarters.

Red Mullet with Capers and Clams

Serves 6

18 ounces (500g) small clams

4 tablespoons salted capers

6 red mullets, about 10 ounces (300g) each, filleted

4 tablespoons olive oil

2 garlic cloves, peeled and sliced

2 dried red chiles, crumbled

4 tablespoons roughly chopped fresh flat-leaf parsley

Pinot Bianco

Soft Polenta (see page 160)

Place the clams in a sink of cold water and wash thoroughly by scrubbing the shells with a coarse brush. Discard any clams that remain open. Soak in clean water, changing the water until it is clear.

Put the capers in a sieve and rinse under cold running water. Leave to soak in cold water for 40 minutes, then rinse again.

Season the fish. In a pan large enough to hold the fillets flat in one layer, heat the olive oil and sauté the garlic until soft but not brown. Add the chiles, capers and half of the parsley, followed by the red mullet fillets with a splash of wine. Cover the pan and cook for 1 minute.

Add the clams with another splash of wine and the rest of the parsley. Cover and cook until the clams are open, about a further 5 minutes.

Serve with soft polenta.

The River Café

Wednesday 11th November

Antipasti

Puntarelle alla Romana

Seppia – cuttlefish slow-cooked in ink with soft polenta

Antipasti – buffalo mozzarella, Italian spinach and bruschetta with
first-of-the-season I Canonici olive oil

Prosciutto e Coppa di Parma – with artichoke alla Romana

Primi

Tagliatelle al Pomodoro

Panzotti – with buffalo ricotta, Venetian pumpkin and marjoram

Taglierini – with Devon crab, chilli, fennel herb and lemon

Fusilli – with Middle White Pork slow-cooked in milk, sage and bay

Secondi

Piccione al forno – half Anjou pigeon wood-roasted in Fontodi Chianti Classico
with Castelluccio lentils and cavolo nero

Branzino ai ferri – chargrilled wild Sea Bass with Amalfi lemon and
potatoes, trompettes de la mort & parsley al forno

Coda di Rospo al forno – Monkfish roasted with anchovies, capers, olives, fennel herb
& Terlano Pinot Bianco with chickpeas & swiss chard

Coscia d'Agnello ai ferri – chargrilled leg of Lamb with fresh horseradish
and wood-roasted pumpkin, Florence fennel & trevise

Dolci

Chocolate Nemesis —— Pear & Almond Tart —— Hazelnut Ice Cream

Peter Doig

Sea Bass Baked in Salt

Serves 4

1 lemon, sliced

a small handful of dried fennel stalks

one 4-pound (1.8kg) sea bass, cleaned and gilled but not scaled

8 pounds (3.6kg) sea salt

Salsa Verde (see page 223)

Preheat the oven to 400°F (200°C).

Put the lemon slices and dried fennel stalks inside the cavity of the fish.

Place the salt in a large bowl and add 9 fluid ounces (250ml) water. Line a baking sheet with parchment paper and cover it with half of the salt. Lay the fish on top. Cover the fish completely with the remaining salt.

Bake the fish in the hot oven. After 20 minutes, insert a skewer into the fish. If the tip of the skewer feels very hot when pulled out, the fish is ready.

Crack open the salt crust and remove the hard pieces, ensuring that no salt remains on the flesh of the fish. Carefully lift the fish and place on a platter. Remove the skin.

Serve warm with salsa verde.

Poached Turbot Tranche

Serves 4

1½ cups (375ml) Pinot Bianco

2 bay leaves

1 bunch of fresh flat-leaf parsley

2 garlic cloves, peeled

peel of 1 lemon

1 teaspoon black peppercorns

four 10-ounce (300g) slices of turbot on the bone

extra virgin olive oil

The last words of Ruthie's Italian mother-in-law, Dada Rogers, to her were "Put more cream on your face and fewer herbs on your fish."

There are no herbs on this fish.

Pour 8½ cups (2 liters) of water into a wide pot and add the wine, bay leaves, parsley, garlic, lemon peel and peppercorns. Salt well, then bring to the boil and simmer, uncovered, for 30 minutes.

Add the turbot to the pot, in one layer, with more water if the fish is not covered by three-quarters. Bring to the boil, then cover the pot and reduce the heat. Simmer for 5 minutes. Remove the covered pot from the heat and leave the turbot undisturbed for a further 10 minutes.

Serve with extra virgin olive oil and a cold anchovy sauce.

Dover Sole with Capers and Marjoram

Serves 6

2 tablespoons salted capers

extra virgin olive oil

1 bunch of fresh marjoram leaves

4 whole Dover sole, weighing 12–14 ounces (350–400g) each, scaled and cleaned

1 lemon, cut in half

Put the capers in a sieve and rinse under cold running water. Leave to soak in cold water for 40 minutes, then rinse again.

Preheat the oven to 450°F (230°C).

Brush a large, flat baking sheet with extra virgin olive oil. Scatter half of the marjoram leaves over the sheet along with some sea salt and black pepper. Place the fish on top, side by side. Season them with sea salt and black pepper, then scatter the remaining marjoram and the capers over them. Drizzle generously with olive oil.

Bake for 15–20 minutes—test with the point of a sharp knife inserted into the center of the thickest part of the sole; if cooked, the flesh should come away from the bone.

Squeeze the lemon over the fish and serve with any juices from the pan and extra olive oil.

Grilled Sea Bass Fillets

Serves 6

one 6¾-pound (3kg) sea bass

1 tablespoon olive oil

3 lemons, cut in half

This recipe, from the blue book, simply explains how to prepare a whole sea bass for grilling—should you ever catch one.

Prepare the sea bass by snipping off the side and back fins with a strong pair of scissors. With a fish scaler or large, strong knife, scrape off the scales. This is best done by holding the fish by the tail in a sink and scraping downward. It is essential to do this thoroughly. Gut the fish by running a sharp knife up from the base of the belly to the head. Remove the guts and wash the fish well.

To cut into fillets, lay the fish on its side and, using a sharp filleting knife, carefully slice along the backbone, from tail to head, keeping close to the bones with the blade so as not to waste any flesh. Then cut downward around the head, which will enable you to remove the fillet. Repeat this on the other side of the fish.

Place the fillets, skin side down. Run your fingers over them to check for any bones. Pull out any that remain using tweezers. Cut each fillet into three portions.

Heat a charcoal fire in the barbecue or a char-grill/griddle pan until very hot. Lightly brush the pieces of fish with olive oil and season well with sea salt and black pepper. Grill over charcoal or on a hot char-grill/griddle pan for about 3 minutes on each side or until cooked. Serve with the lemon halves.

Squid with Anchovies and Peas

Serves 6

6 medium squid (no bigger than your hand)

1 garlic clove, peeled

10 ounces (300g) podded fresh peas

olive oil

1 dried red chile, crumbled

6 tablespoons Salsa Calda d'Acciughe (see page 226)

2 tablespoons chopped fresh flat-leaf parsley

Clean each squid by cutting the body open to make a flat piece and scraping out the guts. Keep the tentacles in their bunches but remove the eyes and mouth. Using a serrated knife, score the inner side of the flattened squid body with parallel lines ½ inch (1cm) apart, and then lines equally apart the other way to make crosshatching.

Bring a pot of water to the boil with the garlic. Add the peas and cook for 5 minutes or until tender. Remove with a slotted spoon to a bowl, season and cover with olive oil.

Heat the grill or a char-grill/griddle pan (or a heavy skillet with a thimble of oil). Place the squid (including the tentacles), scored side down, on the very hot grill and grill for 1–2 minutes. Turn the squid pieces over; they will immediately curl up, by which time they will be cooked. Cut the tentacles in half and the bodies into four.

Toss the squid with the chile, peas, anchovy sauce and parsley and serve at once.

Roast Monkfish with Tomatoes and Oregano

Serves 4

four 7-ounce (200g) monkfish fillets, skinned and trimmed

3 salted anchovies

extra virgin olive oil

10 ounces (300g) yellow and red Datterini or grape tomatoes

3½ ounces (100g) black olives, pitted

Vermentino

fresh marjoram and oregano leaves

Preheat the oven to its highest temperature.

Pat the monkfish fillets dry with paper towels and season all over with sea salt and black pepper.

Rinse the anchovies under cold running water to remove all the salt, then gently remove the spine bones and heads. Pat dry. Separate the anchovies into fillets.

Heat 3 tablespoons of extra virgin olive oil in an ovenproof pan. Add the fish to the pan, shaking the pan to prevent the fish from sticking. Add the tomatoes, olives and anchovies. Season well.

After about 2 minutes, when the fish is lightly browned, turn the fillets over and nestle the tomatoes between them. Sprinkle with some seasoning and an extra drizzle of olive oil, then place the pan in the oven to cook for 5 minutes.

Check the monkfish is cooked with a metal skewer—it should pass through the fish with little resistance. Add a splash of wine to the pan. Sprinkle the herbs over the top and serve immediately.

Ligurian Fish Stew

Serves 6

18 ounces (500g) monkfish or turbot fillets (and bones for stock)

4¼ cups (1 liter) Fish Stock (see page 157)

12 langoustines

¾ cup (175ml) olive oil

3 garlic cloves, peeled and cut into slivers

1 fresh red chile, seeded and chopped

2 fennel bulbs, sliced, green leaves and stalks for stock

2½ teaspoons (10g) fennel seeds

36-ounce (1kg) jar peeled plum tomatoes, drained of most of their juices, sieved

1 cup (250ml) dry white wine

three 8-ounce (225g) red mullet fillets, scaled and pinboned

6 scallops, trimmed

18 ounces (500g) small clams, washed

6 slices ciabatta bread, cut at an angle

1 garlic clove, peeled and halved

1 bunch of fresh flat-leaf parsley

extra virgin olive oil

Cut the monkfish or turbot into medium-sized pieces.

Bring the fish stock to the boil and add the langoustines. Poach for 2 minutes, remove and cool, reserving the stock.

For the tomato base, heat the olive oil in a large saucepan and sauté the garlic, chile, fennel and fennel seeds for a few minutes. Add the sieved tomatoes and wine.

Cook, uncovered, over a gentle heat for about 45 minutes or until thick and smooth, stirring occasionally. Season to taste with sea salt and black pepper.

Add the fish stock and bring to the boil. Now add the mullet, monkfish or turbot and scallops to the soup and bring back to the boil. Add the clams, cover with the lid and cook for 4 minutes or until all the shells are open. Discard any unopened clams. Remove from the heat and add the langoustines.

To make the crostini, toast the bread on both sides and rub with the garlic. Put one crostino on each serving of stew, sprinkle with the chopped parsley and drizzle extra virgin olive oil on top.

Scallops with Sage and Capers

Serves 6

1 tablespoon salted capers

olive oil

24 medium scallops, trimmed

1 bunch of fresh sage leaves

juice of 1 lemon

Put the capers in a sieve and rinse under cold running water. Leave to soak in cold water for 40 minutes, then rinse again.

Coat a skillet with a little olive oil, to prevent the scallops from sticking, and place over a high heat. When smoking, add the scallops, season with a little sea salt and black pepper, and cook for 2 minutes on one side.

Turn the scallops over and immediately add the capers and sage leaves to the pan, plus a little extra olive oil so that the sage leaves fry. Cook for a further 2 minutes, shaking the pan constantly. Squeeze in the juice of the lemon and serve.

Carne

Beef Fillet with Salmoriglio

Serves 6 (or 10 as antipasti)

one 4½-pound (2kg) fillet of beef, trimmed

Salmoriglio (see page 224), made with thyme

7 ounces (200g) arugula

Oil and Lemon Dressing (see page 37)

Prepare a charcoal fire in a barbecue or heat a char-grill/griddle pan until very hot. Rub the fillet with sea salt and black pepper, then briefly grill, turning continuously to blacken the outsides, but making sure that the center remains raw. Leave to cool.

Slice the cold fillet on a board into ¼-inch (6mm) slices. Using a large, pointed cooking knife, press and spread the slices to make them thin and lacy. The grilled edges will hold the pieces together.

Spread out the slices on the plates and spoon the thyme sauce over them. Lightly toss the arugula with the dressing in a bowl and serve with the beef.

Veal Shank Slow-cooked with Barolo and Sage

Serves 6–8

2 veal shanks, about 54 ounces (1.5kg) each, trimmed of excess fat

extra virgin olive oil

1 bunch of fresh sage leaves

4 bay leaves

4 garlic cloves, peeled

1 bottle (750ml) Barolo

9 ounces (250g) peeled plum tomatoes from a jar, drained of their juices

The longer this cooks the better—in The River Cafe we often serve this simply with bruschetta.

Preheat the oven to 400°F (200°C).

Heat an ovenproof pot or flameproof casserole (that has a lid) over a high heat. Meanwhile, season the shanks generously with sea salt and black pepper. Carefully add 5 tablespoons of extra virgin olive oil and the shanks to the hot pot and fry until golden brown all over, turning the shanks every few minutes.

Add the sage leaves, bay leaves and garlic. Sizzle for a few seconds, then pour in the wine. Arrange the shanks so that the exposed bone side is facing down. Add the tomatoes, broken up a little. Cover with a sheet of parchment paper and then the lid. Transfer the pot to the oven.

After 1 hour, turn the shanks over and reduce the oven temperature to 300°F (150°C). Cover the pot again and cook for a further 2 hours, basting the shanks with the roasting liquid a couple of times to keep the meat moist. The veal shanks are ready when the meat threatens to fall away from the bone. Serve with the marrow from the bone and some of the roasting liquid.

Sweetbread Fritto Misto

Serves 6

3⅓ pounds (1.5kg) sweetbreads

2 ounces (50g) salted capers

4¼ cups (1 liter) Chicken Stock
(see page 156)

2 tablespoons red
wine vinegar

1 sprig each of fresh
bay, thyme and sage

3 garlic cloves,
peeled

2 teaspoons kosher
salt

5⅔ quarts (5 liters)
sunflower oil

10 ounces (300g)
semolina flour

10 ounces (300g)
pasta flour or
all-purpose flour

2¼ cups (500ml)
milk

1 bunch of fresh sage
leaves

2 lemons, cut
into wedges

Soak the sweetbreads in cold water for a couple of hours to remove any impurities, then drain.

Put the capers in a sieve and rinse under cold running water to remove excess salt, then soak in fresh water for 40 minutes. Rinse again.

Place the sweetbreads in a pot with the chicken stock, red wine vinegar, fresh bay, thyme and sage sprigs, garlic and salt. Bring up to a gentle simmer over a medium heat and simmer for 3–4 minutes. Remove from the heat and leave the sweetbreads to cool in the liquor.

Once the sweetbreads are cool, remove them from the liquor (discard this) and peel off the outer membrane using your fingers.

Heat the sunflower oil in a large pot or deep-fat fryer to 350°F (180°C).

Mix together the semolina and pasta/all-purpose flour and season with sea salt and black pepper. One at a time, dip the sweetbreads first in the milk, then transfer to the flours and turn to coat. Shake off any excess flour.

Gently place the sweetbreads into the hot oil and fry until golden brown. Just before you take the sweetbreads out of the oil, throw in the capers and sage leaves. The sage and capers will go crispy. Drain everything on paper towels. Serve with wedges of lemon and more sea salt.

Marinated Grilled Lamb

Serves 6

5 garlic cloves, peeled and crushed

2 tablespoons chopped fresh rosemary leaves

a good pinch of coarsely ground black pepper

1 leg of spring lamb, about 5 pounds (2.25kg) in weight, boned and butterflied

2 tablespoons fresh lemon juice

3 tablespoons olive oil

1 tablespoon sea salt

Salsa Verde (see page 223) or fresh horseradish sauce, for serving

Mix together the crushed garlic, rosemary and black pepper in a small bowl. Rub into the cut side of the meat. Place the meat in a shallow dish and pour over the lemon juice and olive oil. Turn the meat over a couple of times to make sure it is coated, then cover and leave to marinate at room temperature overnight, or for at least 4 hours, turning the meat occasionally.

Prepare a charcoal fire in a barbecue or heat a large char-grill/griddle pan until very hot. Remove the meat from the marinade and pat dry. Season with the salt. Carefully place the meat on the grill and brown on both sides.

Lower the heat and continue to grill until the meat reaches the desired degree of pinkness, turning once. Allow at least 8 minutes per side. Rest before serving with Salsa Verde (see page 223) or fresh horseradish sauce.

Pan-fried Calf's Liver with Cavolo Nero

Serves 2

Braised Cavolo Nero (see page 258), to serve

2 thick slices calf's liver

1 tablespoon extra virgin olive oil

¼ cup (50ml) balsamic vinegar

¼ cup (50ml) crème fraîche

Cook the cavolo nero (Tuscan kale) and keep warm.

Season the liver on both sides with sea salt and black pepper. Brush a large skillet with the extra virgin olive oil and, when very hot, fry the liver for 1 minute on each side. Add the balsamic vinegar and turn the liver so that it absorbs the vinegar, which will reduce almost immediately. Add the crème fraîche and let it just melt into the vinegar.

Remove the liver and serve on top of the cavolo nero, with some of the sauce from the skillet.

The River Café

Aperitivo –
Prosecco with fresh
Blood Orange £12

Tuesday 26ᵗʰ January

Antipasti

Calamari ai ferri – chargrilled squid with fresh red chilli & rocket
Mozzarella di Bufala – with Violetta artichoke alla Romana, spinach and marinated black olives
Salumi Misti – with finely sliced Florence fennel & Parmigiano Reggiano
Insalata Invernale – winter salad with rocket, dandelion, warm walnuts and Pecorino

Pasta

Spaghetti – with chopped mussels, parsley, chilli, and Terlano Pinot Bianco
Tagliatelle – fresh hand-cut pasta with Prosciutto di Parma, cream & rosemary
Ravioli – fresh pasta with buffalo ricotta, borrana & cicoria and sage butter

Secondi

Capesante in padella – seared Scottish scallops with dried chilli, chickpeas,
Verdicchio 'Solosole' and roasted treviso
Triglia alla griglia – chargrilled Red Mullet with large leaf rocket and two crostini
of anchovy and black olives
Coscia d'Agnello ai ferri – chargrilled marinated leg of lamb with swiss chard,
roast Venetian squash and fresh horseradish
Fegato di Vitello in padella – pan-fried Calves liver with sage, capers,
potatoes & radicchio

Dolci

Polenta Cake with Caramelised Blood Oranges   Pear & Almond Tart
Roasted Almond Ice Cream   Affogato with Espresso

Peter Doig

Pork Cooked in Milk

Serves 6

one 4½-pound (2kg) boned pork loin, rind and most of the fat removed

2 tablespoons olive oil

¼ cup (50g) unsalted butter

5 garlic cloves, peeled and halved

a large handful of fresh sage leaves

6⅓ cups (1.5 liters) milk

pared rind of 3 lemons, pith removed

Generously season the pork on all sides. Heat the olive oil in a saucepan (with a lid) that is just large enough to hold the pork. Brown the meat on all sides, then remove. Pour away the fat.

Melt the butter in the pan and add the garlic with the sage leaves. Before the garlic begins to color, return the pork to the pan. In a separate pan, heat the milk to warm but not boiling, and add enough milk to come three-quarters of the way up the pork. Bring gently to the boil. Add the lemon rind and reduce the heat. Place the lid on the pan, slightly askew, and very slowly simmer for about 2 hours. Resist the temptation to disturb the meat.

When the pork is cooked, the milk will have curdled into beige nuggets. Carefully remove the meat, slice quickly and spoon the sauce over.

Aperitivo -
Prosecco with fresh
Blood Orange £12

Tuesday 14th March

Antipasti
Ricotta di Bufala al forno – baked buffalo ricotta with herbs, black olives and whole Artichoke sott'olio
Granchio – fresh devon crab with puntarelle & grumolo salad with aioli
Carne Cruda di Vitello – finely chopped veal with lemon and parmesan
Prosciutto di San Daniele & Finocchiona – with rosemary farinata

Primi
Ribollita – Tuscan bread soup with borlotti, cavolo nero, tomato and I Canonici olive oil
Taglierini – treviso, pancetta, thyme, Terlaner Pinot Bianco & parmesan
Orecchiette – with cima di rape, anchovy, chilli and Pangrattato

Secondi
Triglia al forno – wood-roasted whole red mullet stuffed with rosemary with poatoes, olives, lemon, capers & wild oregano al forno
Coda di Rospo – monkfish roasted with salted anchovy & wild fennel with erbette saltate of chard, rocket, cicoria and spinach
Coscia d'Agnello ai Ferri – chargrilled marinated leg of lamb with salsa verde and slow cooked Florence fennel
Maiale al Latte – Middlewhite pork slow cooked with lemon & sage with slow cooked peas

Dolci
Lemon Tart Chocolate, Hazelnut & Espresso Cake   Affogato & Espresso

Aperitivo -
Prosecco with fresh
Blood ... £12

Wednesday 15th March – Lunch

Antipasti

Puntarelle alla Romana £20

Pizzetta – ...oletta arti... Taleggio, thy... capers £21
...amari ai ... chargrilled ... h fresh re... rocket ...
...sciutto di Par... with radicc... onese & fenn... farinata ...
Mozzarella di Bufala – with new season's broad beans, cicoria & black olives £21
Capesante in padella – scallops seared with Merinda winter tomatoes & borlotti di Lamon £22

Primi

Spaghet... ...th Devon C... ...illi, lemon & ... £23
...ini al Pom... fresh fine ... th slow-coo... ...ese tomat...
Fettu... – hand-cut w... ...ers cooked in ... Chianti Class... ...incetta & ros... £22

Secondi

Rombo cotta in bianco – poached Turbot tranche with scottish sea kale
and Sardinian bottarga £42
...liola al for... ...ole Dover Sol... ...oasted with ...am & cape...
wit... ...hio di Tre... ...stelluccio ... 40
...di Rospo – ch... ...led Cornish M... ...ish with anch... ...nd rosemary ...
and braised cima di rape £38
Coscia d'Agnello ai ferri – chargrilled marinated leg of lamb with inzimino
of chickpeas. Pinot Bianco, swiss chard, chilli & tomato £37
...al forno – ... ...jou Pigeon ... ...asted in Ch... ...ith braised ...
...ze and Sp... ...Val d'Aost...
Fegato di Vi... in padella – ... Liver seared w... ...sage & lemon,
with slow-cooked spring peas & Italian spinach £37

Damien Hirst

Braised Beef Fillet

Serves 6

one 4½-pound (2kg) fillet of beef, trimmed of all fat

3 garlic cloves, peeled and cut into fine slivers

a handful of fresh rosemary leaves, plus 6 sprigs

10 ounces (300g) coppa di Parma, sliced thinly

2 tablespoons olive oil

¼ cup (50g) unsalted butter

1 bottle (750ml) Brunello di Montalcino

In the winter, we serve this with polenta (see page 160), butter and Parmesan.

With a sharp knife, make small incisions all over the fillet following the grain of the meat. Into each incision insert a sliver of garlic with a few rosemary leaves and sea salt and black pepper.

Now carefully wrap the fillet from end to end with the coppa slices, slightly overlapping them, and tie on evenly with string, keeping the string turns close together, tucking in the rosemary sprigs. You may not use all the coppa, in which case cut the remainder into slivers.

In a saucepan just large enough to hold the fillet, heat the olive oil and butter and gently brown the wrapped fillet on all sides. Add enough wine to come a third of the way up the sides of the fillet. Bring to the boil, then reduce the heat and cover with a piece of parchment paper. Put on the lid, slightly askew. Simmer gently for 15–20 minutes. Test by pressing the fillet—if it gives gently to your touch, it will be rare.

Remove the fillet from the pan. The sauce should be quite dense; if too thin, reduce over a fierce heat. Check for seasoning. Untie the string, slice the fillet and spoon the juices over.

Pork Braised with Vinegar

Serves 6

one 4½-pound (2kg) boned shoulder of pork, rind and most of the fat removed

2 tablespoons olive oil

⅔ cup (150ml) red wine vinegar

⅔ cup (150ml) Chianti Classico

1 tablespoon black peppercorns

12 fresh bay leaves

Generously season the pork with sea salt. In a saucepan with a lid, heat the olive oil over a medium-high heat and brown the meat on all sides. Remove the meat and put to one side.

Pour the red wine vinegar into the pan. Bring to the boil and reduce the liquid by half. Add the wine, 7 tablespoons (100ml) water, the peppercorns and bay leaves and lower the heat to a simmer.

Return the pork to the pan and turn to coat it in the juices. Put the lid on but slightly askew. Simmer very gently for 2 hours, turning the meat two or three times during cooking. If the juices seem to be drying up, add a little more wine or water.

When the meat is cooked (soft when prodded), remove the pan from the heat and let the pork relax for 5 minutes. Slice and serve with the juices and the bay leaves.

Bollito Misto

Serves 8–10

1 small ox tongue

1 bunch of fresh flat-leaf parsley stalks

1 whole head celery for the stock, plus 3 celery hearts, each divided lengthwise into quarters, reserved for the end of cooking

1 garlic bulb, cut in half

14 medium carrots, scrubbed—
4 for the stock,
10 reserved for the end of cooking

4 bay leaves

2 medium red onions, peeled and halved

2 tablespoons black peppercorns

1 large chicken, preferably a stewing hen

2 cotechino sausages or zampone

This was our good friend and agent Ed Victor's favorite dish.

Soak the tongue in cold water overnight. Drain and place in a large saucepan. Cover with fresh water and add half of the parsley stalks, half the celery head, half of the garlic bulb, 2 carrots, 2 bay leaves, 1 red onion and 1 tablespoon of peppercorns. Simmer for 3 hours, uncovered, skimming occasionally, until the tongue is soft and a skewer can be easily inserted. Remove the tongue and place on a board. Peel off the skin.

Put the chicken in a large saucepan and cover with water. Add the remaining parsley, celery head half, garlic bulb half, 2 carrots, bay leaves, red onion and peppercorns, and gently simmer for 1–2 hours. Then 20 minutes before the chicken has finished cooking, add the reserved carrots and celery hearts. Season.

Cook the cotechino or zampone according to the package instructions.

Remove the three pans from the heat and keep the meats in their various stocks until ready to use.

Cut the tongue into ½-inch (1cm) slices, and the chicken and sausages into thicker slices. Arrange on a warm serving plate and pour on some of the strained chicken stock. Slice the carrots and celery hearts and add those too.

Serve with mostarda di Cremona (seasonal fruit preserves) and lentils (see page 259), and Salsa Verde (see page 223), Bagnet (see page 222) or Salsa di Dragoncello (see page 224).

James Bedford

Pheasant with Josephine Dore

Serves 6

12 slices prosciutto or pancetta

3 pheasants, plucked and cleaned

½ cup (120ml) olive oil

½ cup (120g) unsalted butter

6 garlic cloves, peeled

6 fresh rosemary sprigs

10 fresh sage leaves

1 bottle (750ml) Josephine Dore or Marsala

1½ cups (350ml) Chicken Stock (see page 156)

1 cup (250ml) heavy cream

Josephine Dore is an unusual sweet wine from Sicily. We love its name and like to imagine who Josephine Dore was and why this wine was named after her.

Place the prosciutto or pancetta slices over the pheasant breasts and tie on with string.

Heat the olive oil and butter in a saucepan and brown the pheasants on all sides. Add the garlic and herbs. Cook over a medium heat, partially covered, turning the birds frequently, for about 40 minutes, adding the wine and stock in stages: you do not want to boil the birds but braise them in the liquid, which should just cover the bottom of the pan.

Remove the birds and keep warm. If there is a lot of juice, reduce over a high heat, then add the cream. Let it simmer and thicken. Season with sea salt and black pepper. Pour the juices over the pheasants and serve.

Roast Grouse with Pancetta

Per person

5 thin slices pancetta

1 chicken liver,
finely chopped

2 large, fresh
thyme sprigs

1 garlic clove,
peeled and chopped

2 tablespoons (25g)
unsalted butter

1 cup (250ml) Aleatico
di Puglia

1 grouse, plucked
and cleaned

To make the stuffing, cut two of the pancetta slices into matchsticks and mix with the liver, the picked leaves of one of the thyme sprigs and the garlic, then brown in the butter in a small pan. This will only take a few minutes. When a good color, add ¾ cup (175ml) of the wine and boil to reduce a little. Season and cool.

Preheat the oven to 450°F (230°C).

Spoon the stuffing into the cavity of the bird. Place the remaining thyme sprig on the breast of the bird, cover with the remaining pancetta slices and tie on with string, crossing the string to tie the legs together so that the stuffing does not fall out.

Place in a roasting pan and roast for 20–30 minutes, depending on size and how rare you like grouse (we serve them slightly pink). The easiest way to test for doneness is to pull the leg away from the body at the thigh. If still blue, cook for a little longer. Grouse vary in roasting time because they differ so much in size.

Remove from the oven and leave the bird to rest in the pan for 2–3 minutes, then remove and untie the string. Heat the roasting pan over a medium-high heat, add the remaining wine and reduce by half. Return the bird to the pan and turn to coat it in the juices, then serve. This is delicious with Braised Cavolo Nero (see page 258).

For Coppa di Parma and Mostarda stuffing, chop 1 ounce (25g) coppa di Parma into ribbons. Take 4 pieces of fruit from a small jar of mostarda di Cremona and chop. Mix with the coppa along with ¼ cup (50g) fresh bread crumbs and the picked leaves from 1 small sprig of fresh thyme. Season.

Roast Pigeon Stuffed with Cotechino

Serves 6

1 small red onion, peeled and chopped

2 celery stalks, chopped

2 tablespoons olive oil, plus another 2 tablespoons for the roasting pan

½ ready-cooked cotechino sausage

10 fresh sage leaves, shredded

2 cups (500ml) Chianti Classico

6 Bresse pigeons, plucked and cleaned

Preheat the oven to 450°F (230°C).

To make the stuffing, soften the onion and celery in the 2 tablespoons of olive oil for 10 minutes over a low heat. Remove the skin from the cotechino and crumble the meat with your hands. Add the cotechino and sage to the onion and celery and sauté together for a few minutes.

Pour off the fat from the pan, then add 1 cup (250ml) red wine and boil to reduce by at least half. Season with black pepper and allow to cool before stuffing into the birds.

Heat the remaining 2 tablespoons olive oil in a roasting pan over a medium-high heat, then brown each bird all over. Season with sea salt and black pepper. Place the pan in the top of the hot oven and roast for 20 minutes.

Remove the pan from the oven and take out the pigeons. Keep them warm. Pour any excess oil out of the pan, then add the remaining red wine. Over a high heat, reduce the liquid by half, then season with sea salt and black pepper. Pour over the pigeons to serve.

Salsa

Bagnet

Serves 6

1 tablespoon salted capers

3 salted anchovies

2 thick slices stale bread, crusts removed

3 tablespoons finely chopped fresh flat-leaf parsley

1 garlic clove, peeled and crushed

the yolks of 3 hard-boiled eggs

1 tablespoon white wine vinegar

2 tablespoons extra virgin olive oil

¼ teaspoon freshly ground black pepper

Put the capers in a sieve and rinse under cold running water. Leave to soak in cold water for 40 minutes, then rinse again.

Rinse the anchovies well under cold running water to remove all the salt, then gently remove the spine bones and heads. Pat dry. Separate the anchovies into fillets.

Moisten the bread in water, then squeeze out the liquid. Mix the bread with the anchovies, parsley, capers, garlic and egg yolks, using a fork. Add the vinegar, extra virgin olive oil and black pepper.

Salsa Verde

Serves 10

3½ ounces (100g) salted capers

3½ ounces (100g) salted anchovies

1 large bunch of fresh flat-leaf parsley leaves

1 bunch of fresh mint leaves

1 garlic clove, peeled

1 tablespoon red wine vinegar

7 tablespoons (100ml) extra virgin olive oil

1 tablespoon Dijon mustard

Put the capers in a sieve and rinse under cold running water. Leave to soak in cold water for 40 minutes, then rinse again.

Rinse the anchovies well under cold running water to remove all the salt, then gently remove the spine bones and heads. Pat dry. Separate the anchovies into fillets.

If using a food processor, put the parsley, mint, garlic, capers and anchovies into the processor and pulse-chop until roughly blended. Transfer to a large bowl and add the vinegar. Slowly pour in the extra virgin olive oil, stirring constantly. Finally, add the mustard and check for seasoning.

This sauce can also be prepared by hand, on a board, preferably using a mezzaluna.

Salmoriglio

Serves 6

4 level tablespoons fresh oregano leaves

1 teaspoon sea salt

2 tablespoons fresh lemon juice

8 tablespoons extra virgin olive oil

In a mortar and pestle, pound the herb leaves with the salt until completely crushed. Add the lemon juice. Pour the extra virgin olive oil slowly into the mixture while pounding. Add a little black pepper.

Marjoram, thyme or lemon thyme can be substituted for oregano.

Salsa di Dragoncello

Serves 6

¼ cup (50g) salted capers

2 thick slices stale bread, crusts removed

¼ cup (65ml) red wine vinegar

5 salted anchovies

the yolks of 2 hard-boiled eggs

3½ ounces (100g) fresh tarragon leaves, chopped

½–¾ cup (120–175ml) extra virgin olive oil

Put the capers in a sieve and rinse under cold running water. Leave to soak in cold water for 40 minutes, then rinse again.

Tear the bread into small pieces and soak in the vinegar for 20 minutes. Remove, squeeze dry and chop, ideally with a mezzaluna.

Rinse the anchovies well under cold running water to remove all the salt, then gently remove the spine bones and heads. Pat dry. Separate the anchovies into fillets.

Mash the egg yolks with a fork.

Very gently combine the bread, tarragon, anchovies, capers and egg yolks in a bowl. Stir in the extra virgin olive oil.

Salsa di Peperoncini Scottati

Serves 6

6 medium fresh red chiles

6 tablespoons olive oil

2 tablespoons fresh lemon juice

Heat the grill or a char-grill/griddle pan until hot. Grill the chiles until the skin is black and blistered all over. While still hot, seal in a small plastic bag or put in a bowl and cover with plastic wrap. Leave to cool.

Pull the skins from the chiles. Cut them in half from top to bottom and remove the seeds.

Put the chiles in a bowl, cover with the olive oil and season with a little sea salt and the lemon juice.

Salsa di Peperoncini Rossi

Serves 6

4 fresh red chiles, seeded and finely chopped

7 tablespoons (100ml) extra virgin olive oil

Season the chiles with sea salt and black pepper, then pour the extra virgin olive oil over the top.

Salsa Calda d'Acciughe

Serves 6

6 salted anchovies

2 teaspoons finely chopped fresh rosemary leaves

2 teaspoons fresh lemon juice

⅔ cup (150ml) extra virgin olive oil

Rinse the anchovies well under cold running water to remove all the salt, then gently remove the spine bones and heads. Pat dry. Separate the anchovies into fillets.

Place the anchovies, rosemary and a pinch of black pepper in a mortar and pound to a smooth paste with the pestle. Add the lemon juice and stir well.

Gently heat the extra virgin olive oil in a small saucepan and add the anchovy paste. Stir constantly until warm, but do not allow to boil.

Salsa Fredda d'Acciughe

Serves 6

6 salted anchovies

2 tablespoons finely chopped fresh rosemary leaves

juice of 2 lemons

⅔ cup (150ml) extra virgin olive oil

Rinse the anchovies well under cold running water to remove all the salt, then gently remove the spine bones and heads. Pat dry. Separate the anchovies into fillets.

Crush the rosemary in a mortar and pestle. Add the anchovies and pound to a paste. Slowly add the lemon juice, stirring to blend. Finally, add the extra virgin olive oil, a drop at a time, pounding/stirring. When about half has been added, pour in the remainder of the oil in a thin, steady stream, stirring continuously.

Alternatively, you can use a food processor, although this will produce a thicker sauce. Put the rosemary into the processor and chop very finely, then add the anchovies and chop to a thick, fine paste. Pour in the olive oil slowly. Finally, add the lemon juice.

Serves 6

½ pound (225g) Taggiasca or other Italian black olives

1 fresh red chile, seeded and finely chopped

2 teaspoons picked fresh thyme leaves

1 garlic clove, peeled and crushed

½ cup (120ml) extra virgin olive oil

Remove the pits from the olives. Place the olives in a food processor and briefly pulse-chop. Add the chile, thyme and garlic and again briefly pulse-chop—avoid overprocessing and ending up with a paste. Stir in the extra virgin olive oil. Check the seasoning and add sea salt and black pepper if necessary.

Salsa Rossa

Serves 6

1 red bell pepper

2 tablespoons olive oil

1 garlic clove, peeled and finely chopped

1 fresh red chile, seeded and finely chopped

1 tablespoon fresh marjoram leaves

8 ripe fresh tomatoes, skinned, or 18 ounces (500g) peeled plum tomatoes from a jar, drained of their juices

2 small dried red chiles, crumbled

Heat the grill or a char-grill/griddle pan until very hot. Grill the whole pepper until blackened on all sides. Place in a plastic bag and seal. When cool, remove the blackened skin by rubbing the pepper in your hands or by scraping gently with a small knife on a board. Do not worry if it falls apart. Then remove the seeds and core. Resist the temptation to clean the pepper under running water. Chop the pepper flesh finely.

Heat the olive oil in a saucepan and gently sauté the garlic until it starts to color. Add the fresh chile, marjoram leaves and tomatoes. Cook gently for 30 minutes, uncovered, crushing the tomatoes with the back of a spoon, until the tomatoes are reduced. Stir from time to time.

Add the chopped pepper. Season with sea salt, black pepper and the dried chiles.

Contorni

Braised Spinach with Peas

Serves 6

3⅓ pounds (1.5kg) fresh peas in their pods

extra virgin olive oil

1 garlic clove, peeled and sliced

1 dried red chile, crumbled

2¼ pounds (1kg) spinach, washed and tough stalks removed

In Italy no one ever cooks vegetables al dente, only pasta. So rather than just blanching these peas, we boil them long enough so that they almost melt together with the spinach and the olive oil.

Pod the peas, then blanch them in plenty of boiling water for about 5 minutes. Drain, season and toss with a generous amount of extra virgin olive oil while still warm.

Heat 2 tablespoons extra virgin olive oil in a large saucepan with the garlic and chile. When the garlic is golden, add the spinach, stir and cover. Allow the spinach to steam over a high heat, stirring from time to time, for about 5 minutes or until cooked. If excessively wet, drain the extra liquid away. Season, then stir in the peas.

Ellsworth Kelly

Zucchini alla Scapece

Serves 6

3⅓ pounds (1.5kg) zucchini, trimmed

sunflower oil, for deep-frying

2 tablespoons red wine vinegar

1 large garlic clove, peeled and cut into fine slivers

1 fresh red chile, seeded and cut into fine slivers

2 tablespoons roughly chopped fresh mint

Zucchini fried this way are delicious on an antipasto plate or with grilled fish—and even better on their own with a Negroni.

Thinly slice the zucchini into disks: the thinner they are, the crispier they will be when fried.

Heat the sunflower oil in a large pot or deep-fat fryer to 350°F (180°C). Deep-fry the zucchini, in batches, until light brown and crisp, then remove immediately and place on paper towels to drain. Avoid putting too many in the oil at one time as this will cause the temperature of the oil to drop.

Place the zucchini on a large flat plate and drizzle with the vinegar, then scatter the garlic, chile and mint over the top. Season.

Artichoke Trifolati

Serves 4

6 Violetta artichokes with their stalks

juice of 1 lemon (optional)

3 tablespoons olive oil

2 garlic cloves, peeled and chopped

1 tablespoon chopped fresh mint

1 tablespoon chopped fresh flat-leaf parsley

2 dried red chiles, crumbled

To prepare each artichoke, first snap off the stalk. Cut or break off the tough outer leaves, starting at the base, until you are left with the pale inner heart. Cut the artichoke in half from tip to stalk, then remove the prickly choke with a teaspoon. Cut each half into sixths. The slices will discolor but this does not alter the taste. If you prefer, as each artichoke is prepared, you can drop it into a bowl of cold water with the lemon juice.

Heat the olive oil in a large saucepan or frying pan with a lid, over a high heat. Add the artichoke pieces and stir constantly until they are light brown—about 5 minutes. Lower the heat to medium and add the garlic.

When it starts to color, add about 3 tablespoons water and season with sea salt and black pepper. Cover with the lid and cook until the water has evaporated, which will take about 5 minutes.

Add the mint, parsley and chiles and stir.

Chickpeas with Swiss Chard

Serves 6–8

6 ounces (175g) dried chickpeas, soaked overnight

1 large garlic clove, peeled

6 tablespoons olive oil

2¼ pounds (1kg) Swiss chard

1 medium red onion, peeled and chopped

2 medium carrots, peeled and cut into small pieces

2 dried red chiles, crumbled

1 cup (250ml) Pinot Grigio

2 tablespoons Slow-cooked Tomato Sauce (see page 121)

3 handfuls of fresh flat-leaf parsley leaves

2 tablespoons fresh lemon juice

extra virgin olive oil

Drain the chickpeas and place in a pot with fresh water to cover. Add the garlic and 1 tablespoon of the olive oil. Bring to the boil, then simmer, partially covered, for 45 minutes or until tender. Remove from the heat and keep the chickpeas in their cooking liquid until ready to use.

Separate the large stems from the Swiss chard leaves. Cut the stems into pieces the size of the chickpeas. Blanch the stems in boiling water until tender, then add the chard leaves and wilt; drain. Chop the leaves coarsely.

Heat the remaining olive oil in a large pan over a medium heat. Add the onion and carrots and cook slowly for 15 minutes or until the carrots are tender. Season with sea salt, black pepper and the chiles. Add the drained chickpeas, then pour in the wine and reduce almost completely. Add the tomato sauce and reduce until very thick. Add the chard and mix. Season and cook for 10 minutes.

Chop the parsley leaves and add to the mixture with the lemon juice. Serve sprinkled with a little extra virgin olive oil.

Beets with Capers and Thyme

Serves 6

¼ cup (50g) salted capers

3⅓ cups (1.5kg) beets of mixed colors, scrubbed well and rinsed

1 bunch of fresh thyme

garlic cloves, peeled

juice of 1 lemon

¾ cup (200ml) extra virgin olive oil

10 ounces (300g) arugula

Put the capers in a sieve and rinse under cold running water. Leave to soak in cold water for 40 minutes, then rinse again.

Separate the beets into pans, keeping those of the same color together. Cover with water and season with sea salt and black pepper. Add a few thyme sprigs and a clove of garlic to each pan. Bring to the boil, then cook for about 30 minutes or until soft—test by gently inserting a knife. Drain and allow to cool.

When cool enough to handle, peel off the skins—these should come away easily—and slice into rounds.

Gently mix the sliced beets with the lemon juice, extra virgin olive oil and capers. Season. Serve warm with the arugula.

Melanzane al Pomodoro

Serves 6

4 eggplants, trimmed

⅔ cup (150ml) olive oil

2 garlic cloves, peeled and finely sliced

36-ounce (1kg) jar peeled plum tomatoes, drained of their juices

a handful of fresh basil leaves, chopped

Dada Rogers was a great influence on a whole generation of cooks, including Rose and Ruthie. She cooked her tomato sauce slowly for hours in a skillet until the oil came to the top and there was no liquid left at all. This combination of eggplants and tomatoes should be thick and is best served at room temperature.

Cut the eggplants into 1-inch (2.5cm) cubes. Sprinkle with sea salt and leave in a colander to drain for 30 minutes, to get rid of the bitter juices. Rinse and dry well on paper towels.

Heat 3 tablespoons of the olive oil in a large skillet and sauté the garlic until light brown. Add the tomatoes and simmer, uncovered, for at least 40 minutes until very thick.

In a separate large pan, heat the rest of the olive oil until it is almost smoking. Add the eggplants, in batches, and sauté until brown on all sides. Remove the eggplants using a slotted spoon and add to the warm tomato sauce. Season and stir in the basil. Serve at room temperature.

Melanzane al Funghetto

Serves 6

1 tablespoon salted capers

4 eggplants, trimmed

3 salted anchovies

⅔ cup (150ml) olive oil

2 garlic cloves, peeled and sliced

3 tablespoons chopped fresh flat-leaf parsley

Put the capers in a sieve and rinse under cold running water. Leave to soak in cold water for 40 minutes, then rinse again.

Cut the eggplants into 1-inch (2.5cm) cubes, sprinkle with sea salt and drain in a colander for 30 minutes, to get rid of the bitter juices. Rinse and dry well on paper towels.

Rinse the anchovies well under cold running water to remove all the salt. Gently remove the spine bones and heads. Pat dry. Separate the anchovies into fillets.

In a large skillet, heat 7 tablespoons (100ml) of the olive oil. Sauté the eggplants, in batches, until brown on all sides. Remove from the skillet using a slotted spoon and drain.

In a clean skillet, gently sauté the garlic in the remaining olive oil until it starts to color, then add the anchovies. Stir for 1 minute, breaking the anchovies into the oil. Add the parsley and capers followed by the eggplants. Season and serve.

Fava Beans and Pancetta

Serves 4

2 tablespoons olive oil

5 ounces (150g) pancetta, cut into cubes

1 small red onion, peeled and diced

3 garlic cloves, peeled and sliced

1 tablespoon fennel seeds

1 bunch of fresh sage leaves

2¼ pounds (1kg) young fava beans, podded

7 fluid ounces (200ml) Vino Bianco

bruschetta, for serving (see page 44 for details on grilling the bread)

Heat the olive oil in a pan and sauté the pancetta over a high heat for about 4 minutes or until golden. Add the onion, garlic and fennel seeds. Turn down the heat and sweat until the onion is translucent.

Add the sage leaves and then the fava beans followed by the wine. Season. Cover and simmer for about 10 minutes or until the fava beans are soft and the wine reduced.

Serve with bruschetta.

SPUMA DI CASA: ¥8†′16

Martini with
Blood orange
& lemon £4.50

The River Café

Friday 1st March DINNER

Ribollita, soup of Tuscan bread, Savoy cabbage, Swiss chard, plum tomatoes,
& extra virgin olive oil £5.25
Bresaola with arugola, lemon & black pepper £7.00
Salad of red & white chicory with sauce of fresh tarragon & red
anchovies £6.50
Chargrilled squid with fresh red chilli, & arugola £5.75
Fresh cut Buffalo mozzarella with chargrilled radicchio, pine nuts,
sundried tomatoes & bruschetta £6.75
Gnocchi Verde, gnocchi of spinach, ricotta, parmesan, nutmeg & Swiss
chard £6.00

Grilled Seabass with fresh marjoram, lemon & extra virgin olive oil, &
'Carciofi fritti' (deep fried artichoke hearts) £17.00
Panfried freerange chicken, stuffed with rosemary & garlic, with
porri al forno (leeks baked with parmesan) £16.00
Chargrilled scallops with fresh red chilli & Italian parsley, chargrilled
fennel & blue lentils £17.50
Grilled, marinated, butterflied leg of lamb with salsa verde,   £16.00
& new potatoes, field & wild mushrooms & thyme al forno
Panfried calves liver with vintage wine vinegar, with braised
Savoy cabbage & creme fraiche £15.50
Panroasted pigeon with red wine, stuffed with thyme, with wet
polenta & sauce of pigeon livers, plum tomatoes & black
olives £18.90

12 1/2 % SERVICE CHARGE WILL BE ADDED

THE RIVER CAFÉ THAMES WHARF RAINVILLE ROAD LONDON W6 9HA 071-381 8824

Ellsworth Kelly

Artichokes alla Romana

Serves 6

12 small or 6 large Violetta artichokes with their stalks

3 lemons

3 tablespoons finely chopped fresh flat-leaf parsley

3 tablespoons finely chopped fresh mint

1 garlic clove, peeled and crushed with sea salt

6 tablespoons olive oil, plus 1 cup (250ml)

Prepare the artichokes (see Marinated Artichokes, page 35), but leave them whole. Scoop out the choke with a teaspoon. As each artichoke is prepared, place in a bowl of cold water with the juice of 2 lemons.

For the herbs, mix together the parsley, mint, crushed garlic and the 6 tablespoons of olive oil and season well.

Drain the artichokes. Press the herb mixture inside the center of each artichoke.

Pour the 1 cup (250ml) of olive oil into a pot large enough to contain all the artichokes. Put in the artichokes, stuffed side down, jammed together so that they stay upright. Scatter any excess herb stuffing over the top. Add enough water to come one-third of the way up the globes and bring to the boil.

Reduce the heat, cover with a sheet of parchment paper and place the lid on top. Cook gently for about 30 minutes or until the water has evaporated and the artichokes have begun to brown at the bottom and are tender—test for tenderness using a sharp pointed knife. The timing will depend on the size and freshness of the artichokes. You may need to add more water and cook for longer.

The artichokes should be tender and caramelized. Serve with lemon wedges.

Potato and Pancetta al Forno

Serves 6

4 tablespoons olive oil

3½ ounces (100g) pancetta, thinly sliced

2 garlic cloves, peeled and finely sliced

20 fresh sage leaves

2 pounds (850g) Roseval or similar yellow waxy potatoes, peeled

1 cup (225ml) heavy cream

freshly grated Parmesan

Preheat the oven to 375°F (190°C).

Heat the olive oil in a skillet and sauté the pancetta over a medium heat for a few minutes. Stir in the garlic, add the sage and cook for a minute. Remove from the heat.

Slice each potato lengthwise into thin slices. Place in a large bowl and add the pancetta and oil mixture and the cream. Season with sea salt and black pepper, and toss together.

Put into a baking dish, making sure that the potato, pancetta and sage are evenly distributed. Cover with foil and cook in the oven for 40 minutes. About 20 minutes before the end of cooking, remove the foil so that the surface of the potatoes becomes brown. Sprinkle with a little Parmesan 5 minutes before the end.

Green Beans with Parmesan

Serves 6

1 pound (450g) fine green beans, trimmed

⅔ cup (150ml) extra virgin olive oil

juice of 1 lemon

3½ ounces (100g) Parmesan, freshly grated

Bring a large saucepan of salted water to the boil. Drop the green beans into the water and cover the pan. When the water comes back to the boil, remove the lid and cook until the beans are al dente.

Drain the beans and return to the warm saucepan (off the heat) with the extra virgin olive oil. Season with black pepper and the lemon juice. Stir in the Parmesan and keep stirring until the Parmesan begins to go stringy and coats the beans. Serve immediately.

Cannellini

Serves 6

9 ounces (250g) dried cannellini beans or 2¼ pounds (1kg) fresh cannellini beans

1 fresh red chile

1 small garlic bulb, cut in half

1 sprig of fresh sage leaves

6 tablespoons extra virgin olive oil

As long as you have beans (and slow-cooked tomato sauce) in the fridge, you will always have something to eat.

Soak the dried beans in a generous amount of cold water overnight. Drain the beans well, place in a pot and cover with fresh cold water. Bring to the boil. Simmer for 10 minutes, then drain again and return to the pot. Pour in enough fresh water to cover by about 2 inches (5cm), then add the chile, garlic bulb and sage. Bring to the boil and simmer, covered, occasionally removing any scum that comes to the surface, until tender, which can vary from 40 minutes to 1 hour. Remove from the heat and keep the beans in the water they were cooked in until ready to use.

To prepare fresh beans, pod them, then simmer in water, with the garlic bulb and sage, for 30–45 minutes or until tender. Take care not to overcook.

To serve, drain the beans, discarding the garlic, chile and sage. Season with some sea salt and black pepper and cover with the extra virgin olive oil.

Dried fava beans, chickpeas and borlotti beans can all be cooked using the same method.

Braised Cavolo Nero

Serves 6

6 heads cavolo nero (Tuscan kale)

3 tablespoons olive oil

2 garlic cloves, peeled and finely sliced

extra virgin olive oil

Remove the tough center stems from the cavolo nero (Tuscan kale) leaves. Wash the leaves, then blanch in boiling salted water for about 3 minutes. It is important not to undercook. Drain.

Heat the olive oil in a saucepan and gently sauté the garlic. When it begins to color, add the blanched cavolo and season generously. Cook together to blend the garlic with the cavolo for about 5 minutes.

Remove from the heat, drizzle with some extra virgin olive oil and serve.

Castelluccio Lentils

Serves 6

½ pound (225g) Castelluccio lentils

½ garlic bulb, cut horizontally

3 tablespoons extra virgin olive oil

juice of 1 lemon

2–3 tablespoons chopped fresh herbs (oregano, basil, summer savory, mint or marjoram)

Wash the lentils and place in a large saucepan. Cover with plenty of cold water, add the garlic and bring to the boil. Simmer, uncovered, very gently for about 20 minutes or until the lentils are al dente.

Drain, discarding the garlic, and toss the lentils with the extra virgin olive oil and lemon juice. Stir in the herbs and season to taste with sea salt and black pepper. Serve warm.

Tuscan Roasted Potatoes with Artichokes

Serves 8

12 medium Violetta artichokes with their stalks

juice of 2 lemons

2¼ pounds (1kg) Roseval or similar yellow waxy potatoes

10 small garlic cloves, peeled

leaves of 3 fresh rosemary sprigs, roughly chopped

7 tablespoons (100ml) olive oil

Preheat the oven to 350°F (180°C).

To prepare each artichoke, first cut off some of the stalk, leaving about 2 inches (5cm) attached. Cut or break off the tough outer leaves, starting at the base, until you are left with the pale inner part. Then peel the stalk with a potato peeler, leaving only the pale tender center. Trim the pointed top of the artichoke straight across, which will reveal the choke. Cut the artichoke into quarters vertically. Remove the choke with a teaspoon. As each artichoke is prepared, drop it into a bowl of cold water with the lemon juice.

Peel the potatoes and cut into roughly 1-inch (2.5cm) cubes. Toss with the garlic, rosemary and ¼ cup (50ml) of the olive oil and season with sea salt and black pepper. Spread out in a roasting pan and place in the oven. Roast for 10–15 minutes.

Drain the artichokes, then season and mix with the remaining olive oil. Add to the potatoes and roast for a further 15–20 minutes or until the artichokes are cooked and the potatoes are golden brown. Every so often, stir the potatoes and artichokes.

Slow-cooked Fennel

Serves 6

6 fennel bulbs

5 tablespoons olive oil

5 garlic cloves, peeled

In the River Cafe kitchen we all have an opinion on the color of the fennel bulbs—brown or pale—but we agree on the classic rule that they should be cooked long enough so that you can cut them with a fork.

Cut each fennel bulb vertically into eighths. Heat the olive oil in a large saucepan. Add the fennel, garlic and some sea salt and black pepper, and cook over a medium heat, stirring occasionally, for about 10 minutes or until the fennel begins to brown.

Add sufficient boiling water to come barely one-quarter of the way up the fennel, then lower the heat. Simmer, uncovered, until the fennel is very soft, which will take 20–30 minutes. Stir occasionally and add a little more boiling water if necessary, but there should be no liquid at all when the fennel is cooked.

Toasted Tuscan Bread Salad

Serves 6

1 ciabatta loaf

1 cup (250ml) extra virgin olive oil

2¼ pounds (1kg) ripe plum tomatoes

2 tablespoons red wine vinegar

1 garlic clove, peeled and crushed with a little sea salt

a handful of fresh basil leaves

juice of ½ lemon

Preheat the oven to 475°F (240°C), or the highest it will go.

Roughly tear the loaf into long pieces and place on a baking sheet. Drizzle with a little of the extra virgin olive oil and bake until dry and toasted on the outside, but still soft in the center. This will take no more than 5 minutes. Put the bread into a bowl.

Take four of the tomatoes and, using your hands, squeeze them over the toasted bread. Tear up the tomatoes roughly and add to the bowl, too.

Mix together a dressing using ½ cup (125ml) of the extra virgin olive oil, the vinegar, crushed garlic and some sea salt and black pepper. Pour the dressing over the toasted bread and tomatoes and toss.

Skin and seed the remaining tomatoes, retaining their juices. Slice each tomato lengthwise into eighths and add them, with the basil, to the bread mixture. Finally, add the lemon juice to bring out the flavor of the tomatoes, and pour over the remaining extra virgin olive oil:

Slow-roasted Tomatoes with Thyme

Serves 8

3⅓ pounds (1.5kg) cherry tomatoes

2 garlic cloves, peeled and halved

1 bunch of fresh thyme sprigs

olive oil

If the tomatoes are particularly juicy, prick them with a fork before roasting.

Preheat the oven to 300°F (150°C).

Put all the tomatoes in a bowl, season with sea salt and black pepper, and toss with the garlic. Spread out on a baking sheet without overcrowding. Scatter the thyme sprigs over the tomatoes and drizzle with some olive oil. Roast for 1–1½ hours, draining the juice halfway through cooking, until concentrated and dry.

DOLCI
Blood Orange Sorbet
Lemon Tart
Chocolate and Whiskey Ice Cream
Vanilla Ice Cream
Polenta, Almond and Lemon Cake
Torta di Capri
Pressed Chocolate Cake
Pears Baked with Marsala and Cinnamon
Grilled White Peaches with Amaretto
Zabaglione Ice Cream
Strawberry Sorbet
Pear and Almond Tart
Raspberry and Red Wine Sorbet
Pear and Grappa Sorbet
Campari Sorbet
Espresso Ice Cream
Lemon Sorbet
Caramel Ice Cream
Hazelnut and Ricotta Cake
Mascarpone and Lemon Ice Cream
Chocolate Nemesis

Dolci

Blood Orange Sorbet

Serves 10

20 blood oranges

2 unwaxed lemons

7 ounces (200g) granulated sugar

Juice all but one of the oranges.

Cut the whole lemons and the remaining orange into quarters, removing the seeds.

Place in a food processor or blender with the sugar and pulse-chop to a liquid.

Add the orange juice and pulse once or twice.

Pour into an ice-cream machine and churn until frozen. This should be served on the same day that it is made.

Lemon Tart

Serves 10–12

1 recipe Sweet Pastry (see page 297), well chilled

finely grated zest and juice of 7 lemons

1½ cups (350g) granulated sugar

6 whole eggs

9 egg yolks

10 ounces (300g) unsalted butter, softened

Preheat the oven to 320°F (160°C).

Coarsely grate the pastry into a 12-inch (30cm) loose-bottomed fluted flan pan, then press it evenly onto the sides and base. Chill in the fridge for 15 minutes.

Line the pastry shell with parchment paper and fill with raw rice or dried beans (or baking beans). Bake blind for 20 minutes. Remove the paper and rice, then bake for a further 10 minutes or until golden brown. Leave to cool.

Meanwhile, make the filling. Put all the remaining ingredients, except the butter, in a large saucepan over a very low heat and whisk until the eggs have broken up and the sugar has dissolved.

Add half of the butter and continue to whisk. At this point the eggs will start to cook and the mixture will thicken enough to coat the back of a spoon. Add the remaining butter and continue whisking until the mixture becomes very thick. It is important to keep whisking throughout the cooking process to prevent the mixture from curdling.

Remove the pan from the heat and set it on a cold heatproof surface. Continue to whisk until the mixture is lukewarm. Meanwhile, preheat your broiler to full heat.

Spoon the lemon filling into the pastry shell and leave to settle for 5 minutes. Broil until the top is mottled brown—this should take 3–5 minutes. Cool before serving.

Chocolate and Whiskey Ice Cream

Serves 15

7⅓ cups (1.75 liters) heavy cream

2 cups (450ml) whole milk

4 fresh vanilla beans, split lengthwise

15 egg yolks

1½ cups (350g) granulated sugar

16 ounces (450g) best-quality bittersweet chocolate (70% cocoa solids), broken into small pieces

7 fluid ounces (200ml) whiskey

Follow the instructions given in Vanilla Ice Cream (see opposite) for making the custard. When it has thickened, remove from the heat, add the chocolate and stir until it has melted. Leave to cool, then add the whiskey.

Pour into an ice-cream machine and churn until frozen.

Vanilla Ice Cream

Serves 15

7⅓ cups (1.75 liters) heavy cream

2 cups (450ml) whole milk

4 fresh vanilla beans, split lengthwise

15 egg yolks

1½ cups (350g) granulated sugar

Combine the cream and milk in a large saucepan. Scrape the vanilla seeds out of the beans into the pan, using a knife, then add the beans, too. Heat until just below boiling point. Remove from the heat.

Beat the egg yolks and sugar together until pale and thick.

Pour a little of the warm cream into the egg yolk mixture and stir to mix. Return this to the rest of the cream in the saucepan and cook gently over a low heat, stirring constantly to prevent the custard from curdling. When the custard has thickened enough to coat the back of the spoon, strain it into a heatproof bowl and leave to cool.

Pour into an ice-cream machine and churn until frozen.

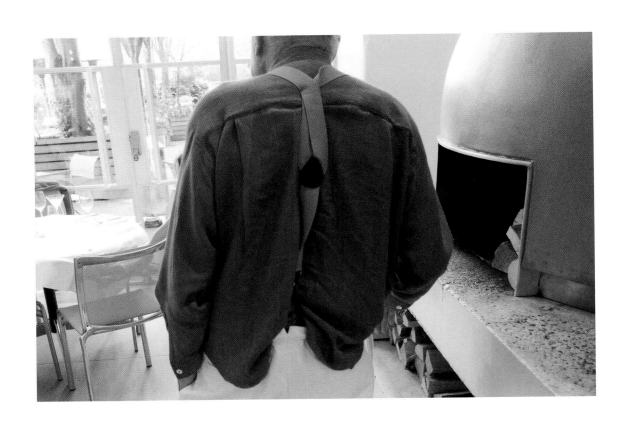

Polenta, Almond and Lemon Cake

Serves 10

unsalted butter for the pan

1 pound (450g) unsalted butter, softened

1 pound (450g) granulated sugar

1 pound (450g) ground almonds

2 teaspoons good vanilla extract

6 eggs

finely grated zest of 4 lemons

juice of 1 lemon

½ pound (225g) polenta

1½ teaspoons baking powder

¼ teaspoon sea salt

*When Richard, opposite, has this cake he pours a glass of grappa over the top.
In Vernazza, we have it for breakfast at Gianni Franzi's with a cappuccino. In winter,
we serve this cake with caramelized blood oranges and crème fraîche.*

Preheat the oven to 320°F (160°C). Butter and line a 12-inch (30cm) round and
3-inch (7.5cm) deep cake pan with parchment paper.

Beat the butter and sugar together using an electric mixer until pale and light.
Stir in the ground almonds and vanilla. Beat in the eggs, one at a time. Fold in the
lemon zest and juice, the polenta, baking powder and salt.

Spoon into the prepared pan. Bake for 45–50 minutes or until the cake is set and
deep brown on top. Cool in the pan.

Torta di Capri

Serves 8–10

unsalted butter for the pan

¾ pound (350g) blanched whole almonds

¾ pound (350g) best-quality bittersweet chocolate (at least 85% cocoa solids), broken into pieces

½ pound (225g) unsalted butter, softened

9 ounces (250g) granulated sugar

5 eggs, separated

Pasticcerie all over Capri serve slices of this torta, and you'll see everyone walking around eating this delicious cake wrapped in a napkin.

Preheat the oven to 300°F (150°C).

Butter an 8-inch (20cm) round, deep springform cake pan and line the base with parchment paper.

Finely grind half of the almonds in a food processor. Pour into a bowl, then coarsely grind the rest of the almonds with the chocolate.

Cream the butter and sugar together with an electric mixer until pale and light. Add the egg yolks, one by one, beating well between each addition, then beat in the ground nuts (both finely and coarsely ground) and chocolate.

In a separate large bowl, whisk the egg whites until they form soft peaks. Fold about a quarter of the whites into the stiff chocolate mixture to loosen it a little, then fold this mixture into the remaining egg whites.

Turn into the prepared pan. Bake for 45 minutes or until set—test by inserting a skewer into the center of the torta: if the torta is cooked, the skewer will come out clean. Cool in the pan.

This cake from Capri is dense, bitter and

It is essential when making this
this cake from Capri is to use
best UN sweetened chocolate which
is only made in In the USA. We
used to have our friends bring in one
in their suitcase but now, happily,
it can be found in shops here.
too It is delicious served warm, and
we slightly undercook it so
that it is very moist—

Char & David Porter

Pressed Chocolate Cake

Serves 10

unsalted butter for the pan

14 ounces (400g) best-quality bittersweet chocolate (70% cocoa solids), broken into pieces

1¼ cups (300g) unsalted butter

10 eggs, separated

1 cup (225g) granulated sugar

4 tablespoons cocoa powder

Preheat the oven to 350°F (180°C). Butter and line a 12-inch (30cm) round and 3-inch (7.5cm) deep cake pan with parchment paper.

Melt the chocolate with the butter in a heatproof bowl set over a pot of barely simmering water (the water should not touch the base of the bowl). Remove the bowl from the pot and cool a little, then whisk in the egg yolks. Add the sugar and cocoa powder and mix well.

In a separate large bowl, whisk the egg whites until they form soft peaks. Fold into the chocolate mixture, a third at a time.

Pour the mixture into the prepared cake pan. Bake for about 30 minutes or until the cake has risen like a soufflé and is slightly set.

Remove from the oven. Place a piece of parchment paper on top of the cake; then place a plate on top of that—the plate should fit exactly inside the pan—and press down firmly, then weight the plate. Leave to cool for 30 minutes before turning out. Cool completely before serving.

We serve this with Zabaglione Ice Cream (see page 294).

Damien Hirst

Pears Baked with Marsala and Cinnamon

Serves 6

6 ripe Comice pears

¼ cup (50g) unsalted butter, softened

½ cup (100g) soft dark brown sugar

¾ cup (175ml) Marsala

¼ cup (50ml) dry white wine

2 cinnamon sticks, roughly broken

crème fraîche, to serve

Preheat the oven to 350°F (180°C).

Cut a small slice from the rounded end of each pear so that it will stand up, then remove the core. Spread a little butter over the skin of each pear and stand them in an ovenproof dish.

Dust the pears with the brown sugar. Pour the Marsala and white wine into the dish. Scatter the cinnamon sticks over the pears, then cover the dish loosely with foil. Bake for about 30 minutes.

Remove the foil and lower the oven temperature to 300°F (150°C). Continue to bake for a further 30 minutes or until the pears are very tender and slightly shriveled. Serve warm with their juices and crème fraîche.

Grilled White Peaches with Amaretto

Serves 6

6 ripe white peaches

1 vanilla bean

2 tablespoons granulated sugar

½ cup (120ml) Amaretto

crème fraîche, to serve

Preheat the oven to 375°F (190°C). Heat a char-grill/griddle pan.

Cut each peach in half, trying to keep the cut as clean as possible, and remove the pit. Carefully place the peach halves, cut side down, on the hot pan and grill until slightly charred. Remove from the pan and place, face up and in one layer, in a shallow ovenproof dish.

Thinly slice the vanilla bean lengthwise and put into a mortar with the sugar. Pound with the pestle until the vanilla bean is broken up and combined with the sugar. Scatter the vanilla sugar over the peaches and pour in half of the Amaretto.

Bake for 10 minutes or until the peaches are soft. Pour on the remaining Amaretto, and serve hot or cold with crème fraîche.

Zabaglione Ice Cream

Serves 10

10 egg yolks

7 ounces (200g) granulated sugar

½ cup (120ml) Bristol Cream sherry

⅓ cup (85ml) Jamaican rum

2 cups (450ml) heavy cream

As an Italian in Britain during the 1940s, Dada Rogers was not able to obtain Marsala for zabaglione so substituted it instead with Bristol Cream sherry and rum. We like it better made this way.

Put the egg yolks and sugar in an electric mixer and beat until light and fluffy—this will take at least 10 minutes. Add half of the sherry and rum, and beat in briefly.

Transfer the mixture to a heatproof bowl that will sit over a large saucepan of boiling water. The water should not touch the base of the bowl. Stir frequently until the mixture comes to the boil—this will take at least 30 minutes.

Remove the bowl from the pan of hot water. Stir the remaining sherry and rum into the zabaglione mixture, then leave to cool.

If you are using an ice-cream machine, add the cream to the zabaglione mixture and churn. If freezing directly in the freezer, whip the cream to soft peaks and fold into the zabaglione mixture, then freeze in a suitable container.

Strawberry Sorbet

Serves 10

2 unwaxed lemons, roughly chopped

2 pounds (900g) granulated sugar

4 pounds (1.8kg) strawberries, hulled

juice of 2 lemons

Put the lemon pieces into a food processor with the sugar and pulse-chop until the lemon and sugar are combined.

Add the strawberries and purée. Add about half of the lemon juice and stir to mix. Taste and add more lemon juice, if necessary—the flavor of the lemon should be intense but should not overpower the strawberries.

Pour into an ice-cream machine and churn until frozen.

Pear and Almond Tart

Serves 10–12

2½ cups (350g) all-purpose flour

a pinch of sea salt

½ pound (225g) cold unsalted butter, cut into cubes

¾ cup (100g) confectioners' sugar, sifted

3 egg yolks

6 ripe Comice pears

¾ pound (350g) blanched whole almonds

¾ pound (350g) unsalted butter, softened

1¾ cups (350g) granulated sugar

3 eggs

For the sweet pastry, pulse the flour, salt and butter in a food processor until the mixture resembles coarse bread crumbs. Add the confectioners' sugar followed by the egg yolks and pulse. The mixture will immediately combine and leave the sides of the bowl. Remove the pastry, wrap in plastic wrap and chill in the fridge for at least an hour.

Preheat the oven to 320°F (160°C).

Coarsely grate the pastry into a 12-inch (30cm) loose-bottomed fluted flan pan, then press it evenly onto the sides and base. Chill for 15 minutes.

Line the pastry shell with parchment paper and fill with raw rice or dried beans (or baking beans), then bake blind for 20 minutes or until very light brown. Remove from the oven, remove the paper and rice, and allow to cool. Reduce the oven temperature to 250°F (130°C).

Peel, halve and core the pears. Place the pear halves, face down and in one layer, in the pastry shell.

For the filling mixture, put the almonds in a food processor and chop until fine. Pour the nuts into a bowl. Put the butter and granulated sugar in another bowl and cream together with an electric mixer until the mixture is pale and light. Add the almonds and beat in, then add the eggs, one by one.

Pour the almond mixture over the pears. Bake for 40 minutes or until the filling is golden brown and set. Leave to cool, then serve.

Raspberry and Red Wine Sorbet

Serves 10

2 pounds (900g) raspberries

1 cup (250ml) Valpolicella

2 tablespoons fresh lemon juice

½ cup (100g) granulated sugar

¼ cup (50ml) heavy cream

Place all the ingredients in a food processor or blender and pulse-chop to a liquid. Pour into an ice-cream machine and churn until frozen.

Pear and Grappa Sorbet

Serves 10

4 pounds (1.8kg) very ripe Comice or Bartlett pears

2 tablespoons granulated sugar

2 fresh vanilla beans, split lengthwise

⅔ cup (150ml) grappa

juice of 2 lemons

Peel, halve and core the pears. Combine with the sugar, vanilla beans and 1 cup (250ml) water in a pan and cook gently until soft. Strain the pears, reserving the vanilla syrup.

Put the pears in a food processor and add the grappa and lemon juice. Purée, then taste and add some of the vanilla syrup to sweeten if needed.

Pour into an ice-cream machine and churn until frozen.

Campari Sorbet

Serves 10

4¼ cups (1 liter) grapefruit juice

2 cups (400g) granulated sugar

7 fluid ounces (200ml) Campari

juice of 2 lemons

juice of 2 oranges

Whisk together the grapefruit juice and sugar until the sugar has dissolved. Add the Campari and lemon and orange juices.

Churn in an ice-cream machine until frozen.

Espresso Ice Cream

Serves 15

7⅓ cups (1.75 liters) heavy cream

2 cups (450ml) whole milk

4 fresh vanilla beans, split lengthwise

15 egg yolks

1¾ cups (350g) granulated sugar

⅔ cup (150ml) double-strength espresso coffee (made from instant espresso), cooled

We tried making this using a cup of espresso made from freshly ground beans but it makes the ice cream too watery. Use instant espresso for the best results.

Follow the instructions given in Vanilla Ice Cream (see page 279) for making the custard. When it has thickened, remove from the heat and pour in the coffee. Stir to mix. The custard should now be a very dark color. Strain into a heatproof bowl and allow to cool.

Pour into an ice-cream machine and churn until frozen.

The River Café

Rossini –
Prosecco with fresh
strawberries £12

Thursday 8th June

Antipasti

Prosciutto e Melone

Calamari ai ferri – chargrilled squid with fresh red chilli & rocket

Mozzarella di Bufala – with zucchini scapece, Risina beans, swiss chard, chilli and basil

Crostini Misti con Ricotta, Fagiolini Verdi, Culatello di Zibello e Aglio

Primi

Summer Minestrone with Pesto alla Genovese

Taglierini al Pomodoro – fresh fine pasta with slow-cooked tomato & basil

Panzotti – fresh pasta with Italian spinach, Prosciutto and mascarpone

Secondi

Capesante in padella – seared scallops with cherry tomatoes, capers,
basil and chickpeas

Coda di Rospo ai ferri – chargrilled Cornish Monkfish with zucchini fritti,
chilli and mint

Controfiletto ai ferri – chargrilled Beef sirloin with summer beets,
large leaf rocket and fresh horseradish

Vitello Tonnato – thinly sliced roast Veal with tuna mayonnaise, Italian spinach,
capers, anchovy & lemon

Dolci

Chocolate Nemesis   Lemon Tart   Caramel Ice Cream

Michael Craig Martin

Lemon Sorbet

Serves 10

4 unwaxed lemons, quartered and seeds removed

2¼ pounds (1kg) granulated sugar

5 ripe bananas, peeled

8½ cups (2 liters) fresh lemon juice

Put the lemons, sugar and bananas in a food processor (it is easiest to do this in two batches). Pulse until the mixture is coarse with very small bits of lemon peel still visible.

Pour the mixture into a large bowl and stir in the lemon juice.

Churn in an ice-cream machine until frozen.

Caramel Ice Cream

Serves 15

6⅓ cups (1.75 liters) heavy cream

2 cups (450ml) whole milk

4 fresh vanilla beans, split lengthwise

15 egg yolks

1¾ cups (350g) granulated sugar, plus 1⅓ cups (275g) for the caramel

Cook the caramel darker than dark. When you think the caramel is getting too dark, keep cooking it and make it even darker until you can't see the pan base underneath and you think you might be asphyxiated by the fumes.

Follow the instructions given in Vanilla Ice Cream (see page 279) for making the custard. Strain into a heatproof bowl.

To make the caramel, dissolve the 1⅓ cups (275g) of granulated sugar in ½ cup (120ml) water in a saucepan, shaking the pan occasionally, then boil until almost black and smoking. Carefully and slowly add this caramel to the warm custard and stir thoroughly. Leave to cool.

Pour into an ice-cream machine and churn until frozen.

Hazelnut and Ricotta Cake

Serves 10

unsalted butter for the pan

9 ounces (250g) shelled hazelnuts

½ pound (225g) unsalted butter, softened

1¼ cups (250g) granulated sugar

8 eggs, separated

9 ounces (250g) ricotta

finely grated zest of 5 lemons

½ cup (65g) all-purpose flour

5 ounces (150g) best-quality bittersweet chocolate (70% cocoa solids), grated

Preheat the oven to 350°F (180°C). Butter a 12-inch (30cm) round cake pan that is 2 inches (5cm) deep, and line the base with parchment paper.

Spread the hazelnuts in a small baking pan and toast in the oven for about 10 minutes or until their skins are loosened. Pour the hot nuts onto a dish towel and rub to remove the skins. Coarsely chop the nuts in a food processor.

Beat the butter and sugar together in an electric mixer until pale and light. Add the egg yolks, one by one, beating well.

In a separate large bowl, beat the ricotta lightly with a fork. Add the lemon zest and chopped nuts.

In a third large bowl, whisk the egg whites until they form soft peaks.

Fold the egg yolk and butter mixture into the ricotta. Sift in the flour and fold it in. Finally, fold in the whisked egg whites.

Spoon into the prepared cake pan and bake for 35 minutes or until set.

Remove the cake from the pan to a plate and leave for 5 minutes, then while it is still warm, cover the cake with the grated chocolate, which will immediately melt.

Mascarpone and Lemon Ice Cream

Serves 15

2 cups (400g) granulated sugar

6 tablespoons fresh lemon juice

20 large egg yolks

5 pounds (2.25kg) mascarpone

Put the sugar and 1½ cups (360ml) water in a saucepan and bring to the boil. Add the lemon juice and stir until the sugar has dissolved and a syrup has formed. Remove from the heat.

Beat the egg yolks in a large, heatproof bowl until pale and light. Add the syrup in a trickle, whisking constantly. Set the bowl over a pot of barely simmering water—the water must not touch the base of the bowl—and whisk constantly until the mixture is thick and creamy. This will take 6–8 minutes.

Remove the bowl from the heat and continue to whisk until cool. Whisk in the mascarpone, then push the mixture through a sieve.

Pour into an ice-cream machine and churn until frozen.

I Dolci   £7

Chocolate Nemesis
Lemon Tart
Almond & Nespoli Tart
Hazelnut & Espresso Cake with Vin Santo Ice Cream
Pannacotta with Grappa and Marinated Prunes
Lemon, Almond & Ricotta Cake
Blood orange sorbet
Caramel Ice Cream

I Formaggi   £7

Moro di Bufala - firm buffalo milk cheese with an olive tree ash & tomato crust from Marche
Taleggio Valsessia - soft cow's milk cheese with a crisp, washed rind from Piemonte
Pecorino Tiu Bore - aged, firm, strong & slightly spicy sheep's milk cheese from Sardegna
Gorgonzola Naturale - soft, fruity & sappy, richly blue-veined cow's milk cheese from Lombardia

Degustazione di 4 Formaggi   £8.50

Please refrain from smoking pipes, cigars & cigarillos

Cy Twombly

Chocolate Nemesis

Serves 18

10 eggs

2¾ cups, plus 2 tablespoons (575g) granulated sugar

24 ounces (675g) best-quality bittersweet chocolate (70% cocoa solids),
broken into small pieces

1 pound (450g)
unsalted butter,
softened

crème fraîche, for
serving

Still the best chocolate cake ever.

Preheat the oven to 250°F (130°C). Grease a 12-inch (30cm) round cake pan that is 3 inches (7.5cm) deep, then line the base with parchment paper.

Whisk the eggs with a third of the sugar with an electric mixer until the volume quadruples—this will take at least 10 minutes.

Meanwhile, melt the chocolate and butter together in a heatproof bowl set over a pan of barely simmering water (the water should not touch the base of the bowl). Remove from the heat.

Heat the remaining sugar with 9 fluid ounces (250ml) water in a small pan until the sugar has completely dissolved to a syrup, stirring occasionally. Gently pour the syrup into the melted chocolate, stirring.

Reduce the speed of the mixer and slowly add the warm chocolate and syrup mixture to the eggs. Increase the speed and continue beating until completely combined. The mixture will lose volume.

Pour into the prepared cake pan. Put the pan into a deep baking pan on top of a dish towel to prevent the cake pan from moving. Fill the baking pan with hot water so that it comes at least two-thirds up the sides of the cake pan. Bake for 1½–2 hours or until set—test by placing the flat of your hand gently on the surface of the cake.

Remove the cake pan from the water. Leave the cake in the pan to completely cool before turning out (don't refrigerate it). Serve with crème fraîche.

Index

Acknowledgments

Georgia Kirsop

Vashti Armit
Matthew Barzun
Sarah Bennie
Jet de Boer
Daniel Bohan
Caroline Butler
Mary Dean
David Douglas Duncan
Tom Downer
Bassam El Jundi
Alice Fisher
Matthew Freud
Roger Guyett
Lucy Harrison
Ian Heide
Laura Higginson
Joanne Holland
Ross Jasper
Norma MacMillan
Yoni Markman
Helen Marsden
Dave McCauley
David MacIlwaine
Caroline Michel
Magdalena Moores

Anya Paul
Charles Pullan
Nina Raine
Stefan Ratibor
Gail Rebuck
Kadee Robbins
Roo Rogers
Luisa Rosario
Linda Saunders
Rae Shirvington
Rebecca Smart
Stephen Spence
Alex Tidey
Pete Valenti
Barbara de Vries
Gary Waterston
Mark Williams
Georgie Wolton
John Young

Richard Rogers
Tilly Trivelli
Jemi Vilhena

and all of the team at
The River Cafe

In 1992, Ed Victor
called and said,
"Ruthie and Rose,
write a cookbook."

This one is for you, Ed.

THIS IS A BORZOI BOOK
PUBLISHED BY ALFRED A. KNOPF

www.aaknopf.com

Knopf, Borzoi Books, and the colophon are registered trademarks of Penguin Random House LLC.

Library of Congress Cataloging-in-Publication Data
Names: Rogers, Ruth, [date] editor.
Title: River Cafe London : thirty years of recipes and the story of a much-loved restaurant / Ruth Rogers, Rose Gray, Sian Wyn Owen, Joseph Trivelli, Matthew Donaldson, Jean Pigozzi, Stephanie Nash, Anthony Michael.
Description: First edition. | New York : Alfred A. Knopf, 2018. | Published in Great Britain under the title: River Cafe 30. | Includes index.
Identifiers: LCCN 2017044066 (print) | LCCN 2017047461 (ebook) I ISBN 9780525521310 (ebook) | ISBN 9780525521303 (hardcover : alk. paper)
Subjects: LCSH: Cooking, Italian—Tuscan style. | Quick and easy cooking. | River Cafe (London, England) | LCGFT: Cookbooks.
Classification: LCC TX723.2.T86 (ebook) | LCC TX723.2.T86 E88 2018 (print) | DDC 641.5945—dc23
LC record available at https//lccn.loc.gov/2017044066

Jacket design by Michael Nash Associates

Manufactured in China

First American Edition